JACKSONIAN DEMOCRACY AND THE HISTORIANS

by Alfred A. Cave

University of Florida Monographs
SOCIAL SCIENCES
No. 22, Spring 1964

UNIVERSITY OF FLORIDA PRESS / GAINESVILLE, FLORIDA

INTRODUCTION

Historians have generally regarded the Jacksonian era as a significant watershed in American political development. Over the years, however, there has been remarkably little consensus in American historiography concerning the nature, meaning, objectives, or long range significance of the Jacksonian movement. The purpose of this brief monograph is to trace the history of this prolonged scholarly dispute over the interpretation of "Jacksonian Democracy." No attempt has been made to offer a definitive interpretation of the party battles of the Jackson period or to pass judgment upon the many diverse interpretations already extant. Rather, the author has endeavored to reproduce—he hopes with a reasonable degree of fairness and objectivity—the interpretive ideas regarding the Jacksonian movement which have been advanced since the appearance, over a century ago, of the earliest scholarly assessment of the Age of Jackson. It is his hope that this modest essay will provide a useful historiographic survey for the student of the Jacksonian era.

Space limitations, as well as the author's intention to emphasize interpretive ideas rather than individual works, have precluded the inclusion of some of the general histories and biographies dealing with the Jackson era which have appeared in print during the last century.

An effort has been made to select for analysis those works which have decisively influenced Jacksonian historiography or which are especially illustrative of a major trend in interpretation. Somewhat more attention has been paid to narrative histories and specialized monographs than to biographies, largely because biographies of individual political leaders of the Jackson era, though often excellent in their own right, have only occasionally provided comprehensive, thoughtful interpretations of the Jacksonian movement as a whole.

The author wishes to acknowledge his special indebtedness to Professor Arthur W. Thompson of the University of Florida, who sympathetically and painstakingly supervised the doctoral dissertation upon which this monograph is largely based. He would also like to express his gratitude to Dean L. E. Grinter and the Graduate Council of the University of Florida for several very generous fellowship grants during his residence at the University. Thanks are also extended to Professors William G. Carleton, Franklin A. Doty and Clifton K. Yearley of the University of Florida, Ralph F. de Bedts of Old Dominion College, Donald E. Worcester of Texas Christian University, Evan G. Coe of Dade County Junior College, Frederic Jaher of the City College of New York, and Philip C. Sturges of the University of Utah, all of whom read either the dissertation or the monograph and were most generous in offering advice, assistance, and encouragement. Finally, my thanks are extended to the Graduate School of the University of Florida for making this publication possible. The author, of course, remains fully responsible for any errors of commission or omission.

ALFRED A. CAVE

Salt Lake City, Utah

CONTENTS

1. JACKSONIAN DEMOCRACY AND NINETEENTH CENTURY HISTORICAL SCHOLARSHIP

The first professional historical narrative of the Jacksonian era was published in 1857 by George Tucker, a retired University of Virginia professor of political economy. A conscientious scholar, Tucker vowed to avoid the partisan's temptation "to represent facts according to his wishes and feelings." He attained a measure of objectivity by recapturing, through lengthy quotations from the source materials, the viewpoint of both the supporters and the opponents of Jackson's administration. However, as a former Whig partisan, Tucker found irresistible the temptation to arraign Andrew Jackson and his cohorts before the bar of history. In his passages of interpretation, he freely characterized the Jacksonians as vulgar political opportunists devoid of principle. Ridiculing the Democratic party of Jackson's era as a grotesque misalliance of "Federalists and Democrats, Bank and anti-Bank, tariff and anti-tariff partisans, friends and enemies of internal improvements," he charged that the only purpose behind the Jacksonian movement was to gain power and spoils by keeping "General Jackson in office and keeping out his opponents." Though he deplored the "singularly unfortunate" effect of Jackson's ignorant "attempts to benefit the currency, the commerce or the finances of his country," Tucker found the greatest Jacksonian disservice to the nation in the subordination of issues to personalities. Under Jacksonian influence, he lamented, the cry "Huzzah for Jackson!" eclipsed all sane discussion of political issues. Arguing that the two party system constituted the nation's primary safeguard to "the highest civil freedom," he deplored this Jacksonian demagogery as a threat to the nation's basic institutions. Mourning the passage of the pre-Jacksonian age of creative leadership, Tucker found the Jacksonians guilty of degrading the nation's political heritage. Characterizing the leader of the Jacksonian movement as a semi-illiterate, bellicose military chieftan unfit for high office, Tucker drew a moral from his study of the Jackson era. The people, he declared in *The History of the United States from their Colonization to the End of the Twenty-Sixth Congress in 1841*, must never again elevate "to the presidential chair anyone who is not generally believed to be conversant with questions of statesmanship."[1]

The protest against the Jacksonian degradation of the Old Republic first given scholarly expression in Tucker's *History* provided the basic theme of most nineteenth-century Jacksonian historiography. This interpretation gained wide currency with the publication, in 1861, of the third volume of James Parton's enormously popular and influential *Life of Andrew Jackson*. Parton's work was curiously ambivalent in its attitude toward Old Hickory and his followers. Though the New York biographer, a former supporter of Henry Clay, appeared personally sympathetic to his subject, there is much truth in John Spencer Bassett's observation that Parton generally accepted, rather uncritically, most of the charges of Andrew Jackson's political enemies, "then disposed of them with a smile." "Under his touch," Bassett noted, "President Jackson becomes the great, well-intentioned doer of most of the politically bad things of the day."[2]

Parton concurred with Tucker in finding Andrew Jackson a presidential incompetent. His "ignorance and passions," Parton wrote, "combined to render him, of all conceivable beings, the most unfit for office. . . . His ignorance of law, history, politics, science, of every thing which he who governs ought to know, was extreme. . . . Andrew Jackson, in fact, was a fighting man, and little more than a fighting man." He concluded his evaluation of Old Hickory's impact upon American political life with a quotation from the

---

1. Tucker, *The History of the United States from their Colonization to the End of the Twenty-Sixth Congress in 1841* (Philadelphia, 1856-57), IV, 22, 56, 139, 288-93. Though numerous political biographies, such as Calvin Colton's *Life and Times of Henry Clay* (New York, 1846), and a few memoirs, such as Thomas Hart Benton's *Thirty Years View* (2 vols., New York, 1854-56), appeared prior to the publication of Tucker's *History*, his work was the first truly scholarly attempt to place the Jacksonian years in historical perspective. The earlier accounts were essentially partisan polemics. The best study of Tucker as an historian is provided in Leonard C. Helderman, "A Social Scientist of the Old South," *Journal of Southern History*, II, 148-63.

2. Bassett, *The Life of Andrew Jackson* (New York, 1935), p. viii; Milton E. Flower, *James Parton, The Father of Modern Biography* (Durham, 1951), p. 59. According to Flower, most of the surviving members of Jackson's administration, many of whom had assisted Parton's research, expressed disappointment and even outrage at his treatment of Old Hickory's presidency. They continued to hope, in vain, that their fellow partisan, George Bancroft, the eminent historian, would one day compose a rival account to counter Parton's hostile image of the Jacksonian movement. Bancroft, however, never provided a comprehensive, scholarly analysis of the Jacksonian era.

English historian, Thomas Buckle: "There is no instance on record of an ignorant man who, having good intentions and supreme power to enforce them, has not done far more evil than good."[3]

Parton's harsh treatment of Andrew Jackson's presidency derived in part from his belief that Old Hickory's forceful use of presidential power threatened to undermine the constitutional restraints upon the Executive. "His will," Parton wrote, "tyrannized . . . over his friends, over Congress, over the country. No Dionysius of old was more the autocrat than he." In larger measure, however, Parton's repudiation of Jacksonian Democracy reflected his conviction that the election of Andrew Jackson symbolized the triumph of a vicious mass of voters who "could see, but not think, listen to stump orations, but not read . . . who could be wheedled and flattered and drilled by any man who was quite devoid of public spirit, principle and shame, but could be influenced by no man of honor." Parton regarded with horror the notion, commonly associated with Jacksonian Democracy, than any citizen is as capable as any other of holding public office. Because of the ascendency of that "pernicious attitude," he wrote, "the affairs of the United States have been conducted with a stupidity that has excited the wonder of mankind." Public questions, Parton pleaded, must not "be left to the wranglings of demagogues, drunkards, savages and madmen." His severest strictures were reserved for the Jacksonian introduction of the "spoils system" into national politics. This innovation, Parton charged, "debauched" the public service and corrupted the Republic. "The government, formerly served by the elite of the nation, is now served . . . by its refuse." The Jacksonians, he concluded, made "pure, decent, orderly and democratic government impossible." Parton's interpretation of Jacksonian Democracy reflected a profound sense of nostalgia for

3. Parton, *Life of Andrew Jackson* (3 vols., New York, 1860-61), III, 694-700. Parton's biography was not the first account of Jackson's career. Numerous Jackson biographies appeared prior to the publication of Parton's work, such as: Samuel Putnam Waldo, *Memoirs of Andrew Jackson* (Hartford, 1817); John Henry Eaton, *Life of Andrew Jackson* (Philadelphia, 1819); Jerome Smith, *Memoirs of Andrew Jackson* (Boston, 1828); William Cobbett, *Life of Andrew Jackson* (London, 1834); Philo A. Goodwin, *Biography of Andrew Jackson* (Hartford, 1832); John Frost, *Pictorial Life of Andrew Jackson* (Philadelphia, 1845); and John S. Jenkins, *Life and Public Services of General Andrew Jackson* (Buffalo, 1850). These were either campaign tracts or accounts of Jackson's military exploits. None included a comprehensive, scholarly interpretation of Jackson's presidency, though some contained sketchy outlines of his career.

the pre-Jacksonian past. Regarding himself as a Jeffersonian democrat, he lamented the passage of the decorous era of Jefferson and
Madison, a time, in his view, when the wise and cultured ruled
the nation and the ignorant and selfish took little part in public
life. Parton joined George Tucker in condemning the Jacksonians
as degraders of the Old Republic.[4]

Despite the severity of his final judgments upon the Jacksonian
influence in American political life, there is a very basic incon-
sistency, or perhaps one might better say, irresolution, in Parton's
interpretation of the Jacksonian movement. In many passages Parton characterized the Jacksonians as the corrupt manipulators of a
vicious rabble; in others, however, they appear as the representatives of the highest American ideals. "Autocrat as he was," Parton
mused, "Andrew Jackson loved the people, the sons and daughters
of toil, as truly as they loved him." While lauding the nobility
of the Old Hero's ideals, he castigated Jackson's political opponents
for their dismal conservatism, their slavish imitation of European
ways, and their lack of comprehension of "the great sentiment
which breathed all the life into this great Republic." Despite his
distaste for the rabble that presumably brought Jackson to power,
he spoke of Old Hickory's election as a triumph of the "people"
over a decadent "silver forked aristocracy." Parton added: "The
truly helpful men and women of this Republic have oftenest sprung

4. Parton, III, 30, 119, 214-21, 695-701. It should be noted that Parton's
conception of Jeffersonian democracy was essentially a conservative one. Though
reluctantly accepting the mass franchise, an accomplished fact by 1860, on the
grounds that the growing enlightenment of the public of his day had finally
made popular sovereignty workable, Parton expressed approval of Van Buren's
opposition to universal suffrage in the New York Constitutional Convention of
1821. "He had the courage and the wisdom to insist that true democracy does
not require that manifest absurdity, which is called 'universal suffrage.'" Parton's comments on the demise of the caucus system of presidential nomination
were also indicative of his conservatism. "While King Caucus reigned . . . the
game was snugger and cleaner than it was afterward, when every political
center in the Union became a little Washington and every drinking house a den
of president makers. Under the old system a man of talent, force, originality,
and sincerity had a chance of becoming President; under the new, all have a
chance except such." On the other hand, however, he did not question the
principle of popular election of the President. He castigated Henry Clay's
refusal to bow to the popular will in the contested election of 1824-25 and
argued that Clay's support of Adams rather than Jackson was proof of his
political unsoundness. "The candidate that had come nearest to an election by
the people was obviously the one for whom a truly democratic member of
Congress would have given his support. All questions respecting the comparative
fitness of the candidates were impertinent." III, 30, 59, 119, 129, 701.

4

from the cabin, and learned to read by the light of pine-knots, and worked their way up to their rightful places as the leaders of the people, by the strength of their own arm, brain and resolution." Did the Jacksonians represent these creative, self-made leaders? Parton never really decided. He could not believe in the wisdom or virtue of many of the followers of Old Hickory, but even less could he sympathize with the supposedly antidemocratic, "aristocratic" prejudices of the Jacksonians' opposition.[5]

One explanation for the ambivalence of Parton's view of the Jacksonians may be found in his fervid belief in laissez-faire economics and Spencerian Social Darwinism. Arguing that freedom could be maintained only by strict adherence to the Jeffersonian and Social Darwinian maxim, "He governs best who governs least," Parton found the "paternalistic" theory of government espoused by the National Republican party and by the Webster-Clay Whigs incompatible with "true liberty." Those who believed that "government should undertake great national works, such as bridges, canals and roads, should found great national institutions, such as colleges, banks, libraries, museums and laboratories," Parton declared, were advocates of a paternalistic despotism. Hailing President Jackson's message vetoing the Maysville Road bill, he wrote: "Would that the principles it unfolds had been permanently adopted! It did vast good . . . in checking the torrents of unwise appropriations, and in throwing upon the people themselves the task of making the country more habitable and accessible." Jackson, he declared, possessed a profound "intuitive and instinctive" sense of sound political economy. Of the opposition program, however, he concluded: "Want of wisdom . . . marked their conduct from the beginning to the end of General Jackson's administration."[6]

Parton's treatment of the Bank controversy reflected both his rejection of the National Republican economic program and his distaste for the Jacksonian party. He was most suspicious of the motives behind the Jacksonian attack on the Bank of the United States. In his view, Jackson was moved by petty, personal hostility to Nicholas Biddle, not by a proper, rational conviction that the Bank's special privileges endangered liberty. His conduct during the recharter debate, to Parton, was but another illustration of the

5. *Ibid.*, III, 148-50, 613-14.
6. *Ibid.*, III, 83, 285-86, 409, 590.

"violence" of his temperament. His supporters, Parton argued, were not really concerned with the dangers inherent in monopoly, but were concerned only with the hope of selfish gain. "The real object of the politicians who influenced General Jackson was not to rid the country of a monstrous monopoly, but to add to the sum, already prodigious and alarming, of governmental patronage." The tenor of the campaign against the Bank he labelled "arrogant, ferocious and mean," compounded of low demagogery and personal spite. He concluded that the charges against the Bank were, for the most part, false. Yet, opposing on doctrinaire grounds all grants of special privilege, he could not endorse Biddle's cause and ended his account of the Bank war by praising Jackson's veto message as a great state paper.[7]

Despite his conviction that most Jacksonian policies were essentially sound, Parton's final judgment of Jackson's place in American history was a highly negative one: "The good which he effected has not continued; while the evil he began remains, has grown more formidable, has not attained such dimensions that the prevailing feeling in the country, with regard to the corruption and inefficiency of the government, is despair." Partially convinced that the triumph of Jackson represented, or at least reflected, the uprooting of a decadent aristocracy unfit to rule, certain that the movement's basic economic principles were wise and sound, he nonetheless could not accept its political implications. He recoiled from the "turbulence" of Jacksonian politics, the corruption of the "spoils system," and the triumph of "majority prejudice," just as he rejected the "arrogance," "selfishness," and "paternalism" of Jackson's political opponents.[8]

Parton concluded his *Life of Andrew Jackson* with an appeal for the emergence of a new cultured elite, devoted to democratic ideals but free of Jacksonian vulgarity. That elite, he wrote, must champion in politics, not "paternalistic despotism," but the "principles of Jefferson and Spencer." With some bitterness Parton declared, "The calamity of the United States has been that the educated class has not been able to accept the truths of the democratic creed."[9]

The Social Darwinist philosophy which colored James Parton's view of the Jacksonian era gained, in the decades following the Civil War, widespread acceptance. The high priest of the cult of Social Darwinism in America was, without question, Professor

7. *Ibid.*, III, 397, 517, 590.   8. *Ibid.*, III, 694-700.   9. *Ibid.*, III, 699-700.

6

William Graham Sumner of Yale University. Sumner, long celebrated for his pioneering work in sociology and anthropology and customarily identified with the conservative tradition in American economic thought, was also an avid and, in some respects, perceptive student of the American past. He brought to the study of history the assumptions and predilictions of a highly dogmatic, intrepidly conservative Social Darwinist deeply committed to laissez faire. His historical writings reflect that commitment.[10]

Unlike Parton, who regarded the principles of Jefferson and the "truths of Spencer" as complementary, Sumner found both the Jeffersonian and the Jacksonian creeds potential obstacles to human progress. Sharing little of Parton's sentimental democratic idealism, he characterized Jefferson as a "womanish" purveyor of "popular platitudes" and dismissed his egalitarian philosophy as a "fantastic, preposterous dogma." In an essay published in 1883, Sumner declared the greatest danger in a democratic state to be the possibility of perverting government into a "system of favoring a new privileged class of the many and the poor." "Let it be understood," Sumner declared, "that we cannot go outside of this alternative: liberty, inequality, survival of the fittest; non-liberty, equality, survival of the unfittest. The former carries society forward and benefits all its best members; the latter carries society downwards and favors all its worst members." In Jeffersonian egalitarianism, Sumner found the intellectual origins of that dreaded perversion. In Jacksonian majoritarian democracy he perceived the beginnings of its implementation.[11]

Perhaps for that reason, Sumner found a special significance in the history of the Jacksonian era. "No period," the Yale professor declared in an address to the Kent Club in 1880, "equals in interest

10. A brief but excellent analysis of Sumner as a social theorist is provided in Richard Hofstadter, *Social Darwinism in American Thought* (Boston, 1955), 51-66. For a more extensive account, see Robert Green McCloskey, *American Conservatism in the Age of Enterprise* (Cambridge, 1951). Also of value are Harris E. Starr, *William Graham Sumner* (New York, 1925); Albert G. Keller, *Reminiscences of William Graham Sumner* (New Haven, 1933); Ralph Gabriel, *The Course of American Democratic Thought* (New York, 1956), chapter 16; Stow Persons, *American Minds* (New York, 1958), 244-50.

11. *Andrew Jackson as a Public Man* (Boston, 1882), pp. 28-29, 255-57; *What the Social Classes Owe to Each Other* (New York, 1883), p. 37; Hofstadter, p. 51. Sumner's *Andrew Jackson* is not primarily a biography of Old Hickory. Less than 80 out of the 386 pages of the first edition are devoted to Jackson's personal career. The remainder deal with the political issues of the first four decades of the nineteenth century.

7

the administration of Andrew Jackson." In 1882 Sumner published a political biography of Old Hickory, *Andrew Jackson as a Public Man*. Much of his interpretation of the Jacksonian movement was derived from his conviction that the coming to power of the masses associated with Andrew Jackson's electoral triumph in 1828 increased immeasurably the ever-present danger that the "unfit" might ban together to use their political power to interfere with the "natural order." Writing of the fondness for inflationary financial measures cherished by many, though not all, of Jackson's supporters, Sumner assailed their use of government to "advance the interests of the classes which have the least money and the most votes." As a hard-money conservative Democrat frightened by the agrarian radicalism of his own day, he lamented the fact that a "democratic republican government" made it possible for a "corrupt majority of debtors" to "rob the minority of creditors." He deemed the "wanton hostility" of the "democratic element" toward their social superiors truly ominous and condemned the Jacksonians for inciting that animosity. Analyzing the Jacksonian agitation against the Bank of the United States, Sumner found opposition to recharter grounded in "ignorance of the realities of money and credit," compounded with political opportunism and mob hatred of the wealthy and prosperous. Because of the triumph of mob prejudice embodied in the Jacksonian crusade, the Jackson administration "unjustly, passionately, ignorantly and without regard to the truth, assailed a great financial institution." Sumner concluded that Jacksonian monetary policies were responsible for much of the economic distress of the late 1830's[12]

Sumner's profound fear of mob rule led to the conviction that both social stability and human progress required restraint of the will of the majority. Finding in the Constitution the restrictions upon the excesses of democracy he deemed essential to order, he

12. "The Administration of Andrew Jackson," *The Forgotten Man and Other Essays* (New Haven, 1918), p. 338; *Andrew Jackson*, pp. 119-35, 224-49, 259-76, 291-321, 336-39. For Sumner's interpretation of Jacksonial banking policies, see also his *History of Banking in the United States* (New York, 1896), pp. 192-218. Though he deplored the Jacksonian assault on the Bank as misguided, demagogic, and purely negative, Sumner was by no means an uncritical champion of Nicholas Biddle. Biddle, he declared, adhered to an "unsound, obsolete theory of government finance." Sumner argued that the Bank of the United States was never subjected to adequate public regulation. Arguing for the necessity of establishing "the authority of the state over banks," Sumner complained that the bankers of Jackson's day "disregarded law so habitually that it became a commonplace that law could not bind them."

8

condemned the Jacksonians as subverters of constitutional restraint. He labelled Thomas Hart Benton's insistence that legislators in a democracy are morally bound to express the majority will of their constituents "an assault on the Constitution." Finding the belief in the absolute sovereignty of the majority "as far removed from constitutional liberty as . . . Louis Fourteenth's saying, '*L'Etat c'est moi*,' " Sumner deplored the fact that this "Jacksonian doctrine has permeated our whole community far too deeply." He concluded that most of the major political evils of his day emanated from that "unfortunate development."[13]

Old Hickory, in Sumner's analysis, provided the mob, impatient of all restraint and jealous of all talent and wealth, with a champion who typified their own deplorable prejudices. "One can easily discern in Jackson's popularity," he wrote, "an element of instinct and personal recognition. They felt, 'He is one of us . . . he thinks as we do'. . . His adherents had a most delightful sense of their own power in supporting him in defiance of sober, cultivated people who disliked him for his violence, ignorance and lack of cultivation." Sumner, foreshadowing, in a sense, Frederick Jackson Turner, regarded Jackson and his movement as an expression of the democratic instincts of Western America. But whereas Turner saw in the West the birthplace of those American institutions which made this nation superior to the Old World, Sumner regarded the frontier as the spawning ground of most of the distasteful aspects of American life. He disliked its agrarian radicalism and he was horrified by the "barbarity" of Western life. He therefore found little cause to rejoice that the Western influence, under Jackson, had triumphed in national politics. The election of Jackson, he complained, "meant that an uneducated Indian fighter had been charged with the power of the presidency."[14]

Despite his extreme distaste for the Jacksonian version of Democ-

13. *Andrew Jackson*, pp. 96-99. And see also, "The Administration of Andrew Jackson," p. 349. Sumner was among the first historians to argue that the Founding Fathers feared democracy and wished to fix stringent limitations upon the rule of the people in the federal structure. This thesis was advanced, three decades before the work of J. Allen Smith and Charles A. Beard, in an essay entitled, "Advancing Organization in America," which, for some reason, was left unpublished during Sumner's lifetime. *Essays of William Graham Sumner* (New Haven, 1934), II, 340-60; Hofstadter, p. 60.
14. *Andrew Jackson* (1882 edition), 6-7, 77-82; *Andrew Jackson* (1899 edition), pp. 7, 179. (All further citations will, unless otherwise noted, be taken from the 1882 edition.)

9

racy, Sumner declared, rather reluctantly, that "it came in Andrew Jackson's way to do some good, to check some bad tendencies and to strengthen some good ones." Judging the statesmen of the past in terms of their strict conformity to the principles of laissez faire, he found certain Jacksonian policies worthy of commendation. The movement's opposition to monopoly and special privilege, its hostility to extensive federal internal-improvement legislation, and its professed belief in limiting the power of government, all were in accord with Sumner's political philosophy. He concluded his account of Jackson's political career, however, by declaring that Old Hickory left "behind him distorted and discordant elements of good and ill, just fit to produce turmoil and disaster in the future."[15]

The polemical tone of his *Andrew Jackson as a Public Man* notwithstanding, Sumner, unlike most Gilded-Age historians, did not rely upon moral judgments alone in his interpretation of Jacksonian Democracy. More sophisticated than most of his scholarly contemporaries, he also sought to analyze the reasons for the growth and vitality of the Jacksonian movement. In his explanation of the origins of the Jacksonian upheaval, Sumner relied rather heavily upon an economic interpretation of history. Declaring that "the causes of the new strength of Democracy were economic," he sought to explain the boldness of the "common man" who sustained the Jacksonian cause in terms of the unprecedented economic opportunities offered the average citizen in an expanding society as yet unstratified by the emergence of a permanent wage earning class. "The conditions," he wrote, "were such as to give to each a sense of

15. *Andrew Jackson*, p. 279, Ironically enough, Sumner, a staunch Gilded Age conservative, was most attracted to that faction of the Jacksonian party which conservatives of the 1830's and 1840's denounced as a dangerously radical menace to organized society. Though he deplored the "egalitarian theorizings" of the Locofocos, he found them free of the corruption which he felt characterized other supporters of Jackson and applauded their strict insistence upon fidelity to the principles of laissez faire. This splinter group, he wrote, "contributed the most to the welfare of the country. Today, the Democratic party is, by tradition, the party of hard money, free trade and the non-interference theory of government. If that theory is traced back to its source, it will lead, not to the Jacksonian party of 1829, but to the Locofocos of 1835," p. 373. In the 1899 edition, Sumner changed that passage to read, "The Democratic party was for a generation the party of hard money, free trade and the non-interference theory of government." *Andrew Jackson* (1899 edition), p. 438. The change was no doubt a veiled reference to the triumph of the inflationist, free-silver wing of the party in its 1896 convention.

room and power. Individual energy and enterprise were greatly favored. Of course, the effect on the character of the people was certain. They became bold, independent, energetic and enterprising." Jackson, in Sumner's analysis, symbolized and articulated this new audacity.[16]

Sumner also found economic factors at the root of many of the partisan battles of the Jackson era. He regarded the struggle over land policies as the product of the determination of the vested interests of the East to restrict Western expansion and Western opportunity so that "lower wages would then suffice to hold laborers in the city." He found the tariff controversy a reflection of the efforts of Eastern manufacturing interests to exploit the Southern agrarian economy. Though strongly disapproving of nullification, Sumner declared the "Southern grievance" to be "undeniable." Not only did he find evidence of both sectional and class antagonisms in the politics of the 1830's, but on most of the issues that reflected those antagonisms, he expressed warm sympathy for the Southern and Western position. He did not allow his sympathy to alter his castigation of the Jacksonian movement, however. He denied that the Jacksonian party expressed these basic conflicts of interest with any clarity or fidelity. The Jacksonian coalition, in Sumner's view, as in Tucker's, was a *mésalliance* of illogical and incompatible elements, united only in a common adulation of the Old Hero and in a common determination to obscure the issues.[17]

In some respects, Sumner's treatment of the Jacksonian era foreshadowed twentieth-century Jacksonian historiography. Many of the major interpretive themes later employed to explain Jacksonian Democracy may be found, in germinal form, in Sumner's life of Jackson. The influence of the frontier, the conflict of sectional interests, the importance of economic and class antagonisms, the amorphous nature of the Jacksonian party, all are discussed, briefly and incompletely, in Sumner's work. Unfortunately, his often acute historical insights were blurred by a propensity to excessive and highly subjective moralizing. Nonetheless, Sumner's study of the Jacksonian era provided the most valuable analysis of the period written during the Gilded Age.

James Schouler's narrative of the Jacksonian years, published in the third and fourth volumes of his *History of the United States under the Constitution*, shed little light upon the questions con-

16. *Andrew Jackson*, pp. 136-38.   17. *Ibid.*, pp. 185-223.

cerning the origins of the Jacksonian movement raised by Sumner. Though Schouler's use of source materials was more extensive than Sumner's (he was the first scholar to make extensive use of the Jackson and Van Buren papers held by the Library of Congress), his interpretation of the Jacksonian movement seldom transcends the level of a partisan polemic. Schouler, the Republican son of a Whig journalist, charged the Jacksonians with responsibility for that "corruption" and "debauchery" in American political life which reached its height in the scandals of the Grant era. "There was a vigorous vulgarity about Jackson's administration at every point," he contended. "The painted Jezebel of party patronage seized upon the public trusts for her favorites. . . . Andrew Jackson was the first President from what we call the masses, the first whose following vulgarized, so to speak, the national administration and the social life at the capital." Of Jackson's political appointees, Schouler declared: "Certainly no list so lengthy . . . with so many mean and even infamous characters had ever before been presented by an American executive." Under Jackson's guidance, the Democratic party, utilizing the methods of spoils-system politics, "became an army of occupation . . . intrenched in office . . . with all the resources of national influence at command to resist, if need be, majorities and public opinion." Though Schouler softened his harsh portrayal of Jackson's presidency by granting that Old Hickory "was honest and upright in the general endeavor to give his countrymen a high and noble administration," he found the Old Hero basically a rude, if honest, demagogue motivated in part by honor but more by "jealousy and the desire for revenge." He characterized Jackson in his use of presidential power "the veriest autocrat" who ever ruled in America. The Jacksonian conception of the presidential office he condemned as potentially subversive of the Constitution. Andrew Jackson's "iron rule," Schouler concluded, ploughed "long furrows in the back of the Republic whose scars are still visible."[18]

Despite the hostile tone of his evaluation of the Jackson administration, Schouler actually differed with the Jacksonians on few

18. *History of the United States under the Constitution* (1885, 1889), III, 455-64; IV, 33, 108-9, 115, 266-73. On Schouler's career as an historian, see Lewis Ethan Ellis, "James Schouler," *The Marcus W. Jernegan Essays in American Historiography*, ed. William T. Hutchinson (Chicago, 1937), pp. 84-101; Michael Kraus, *The Writing of American History* (Norman, 1953), pp. 198-202; Harvey Wish, *The American Historian* (New York, 1960), pp. 213-18.

matters of public policy. Endorsing the Jacksonian espousal of limited government, he followed Parton in arguing that, in the party battles of the Jackson era, "the Jacksonians had the better principles." A professed Jeffersonian, he expressed few of the misgivings concerning the principle of majority rule which permeated the pages of Sumner's writings on the Jackson era. Though he characterized the tenor of the Jacksonian assault upon the Second Bank of the United States as one of unprincipled demagogery and deemed most of the charges against that institution unjustified, Schouler found the Jacksonian position on the Bank issue sound in principle. By Jackson's day, he argued, "the time had come for the United States . . . to break the web of corporate favoritism which was becoming a corded net upon its growing shoulders."[19]

In part, the apparent contradiction between Schouler's acceptance of much of the Jacksonian view of public policy and his extreme aversion for the Jacksonian influence in American politics may be explained by his profound fear of radicalism and class conflict. Schouler followed Sumner in regarding the hatred and jealousy of the poor for the rich as the basic source of Jacksonian political power. A conservative lawyer of Republican political persuasion, he was most alarmed by the demagogic exploitation of these class antagonisms by Jacksonian politicians. He deplored the "general spirit of lawlessness" which, in his judgment, characterized the Jacksonian era. In a passage most indicative of his deepest convictions and prejudices, Schouler lamented the fact that the coming of Jackson was attended by manifestations of "political folly" including "the increasing tendency to popular legislation, such as the abolition of the death penalty, the treatment of crime as a sort of disease to arouse one's pity, the relaxation of all punishment, all restraint." There was little of the reformer in Schouler's temperament. He perceived altogether too much of the reformist spirit in the Jacksonian crusade, and altogether too little respect for the rights of property and the sanctity of the old verities.[20]

However, Schouler's distaste for the Jacksonian movement also reflected preoccupation with the one cause that did command his sympathy, civil service reform. It is most revealing that a dispropriate part of his narrative is devoted to the manifold horrors of the spoils system. The lengthy passages portraying the "reign

19. Schouler, IV, 134-47, 195-96, 260-71.
20. *Ibid*, IV, 69, 71, 201-3, 260-71.

of terror" in Washington which, according to Schouler, followed Jackson's elevation to the Presidency attained an angry eloquence quite out of keeping with the normally pedestrian, somewhat labored, style of his prose. It may be that his concern for the political problems of his own day, his propensity to castigate the Jacksonians for the political sins of the Stalwarts, provides the basic key to Schouler's intense anti-Jacksonian animus.[21]

The publication of the English translation of the second volume of Dr. Hermann Eduard von Holst's *Constitutional and Political History of the United States* offered further support to those American scholars who deplored the "Jacksonian degradation of Democracy." Von Holst based his analysis of the Jacksonian movement upon the premise that "popular sovereignty . . . would be a . . . dreadful condition of things." Stressing that "conservative sense which a democratic government needs more than any other form of state," the Russian-born and German-educated von Holst charged the Jacksonians with the subversion of the institutional restraints upon the "mob spirit" he found embodied in the American Constitution. He protested that the cohorts of Old Hickory "raised the caprice of the majority to the dignity of the sole law of the land." Commenting upon their insistence that Jackson, the popular favorite in the indecisive electoral vote of 1824, was morally entitled to the support of all truly democratic representatives in Congress, von Holst branded their view of majority rule "not a postulate of democracy, but the overthrow of the constitutional state." "In a democratic constitutional state," he argued, "the legally and morally binding rule is not the will of the majority of the people expressed in any way that suits their whims, but the will of the majority expressed in the way provided by the Constitution, and in no other." Denying that the Founding Fathers intended to create a popularly elected chief executive, he warned that acceptance of the Jacksonian interpretation of the democratic principle would lead to anarchy and mob rule.[22]

Von Holst also charged the Jacksonians with endeavoring to transform the President into a "patriarchal ruler of the republic."

21. *Ibid.*, III, 455-77.
22. *The Constitutional and Political History of the United States* (Chicago, 1879-88), I, x, 32, 158-60; II, 8, 77-79; IV, 74-75. A compact summary of von Holst's interpretation of the Jackson era is provided in his *Die Administration Andrew Jacksons in ihrer Bedeutung für die Entwickelung der Demokratie in den Vereinigten Staaten von Amerika* (Düsseldorf, 1874). An excellent analysis

14

Finding Jackson's conduct of the Presidency subversive of the "rule of law," he proclaimed: "Since Louis XIV, the maxim, '*L'etat c'est moi*' has scarcely found, a second time, so ingenuous and complete an expression as in Andrew Jackson." He found the source of that Jacksonian despotism in Old Hickory's claim to be the "direct representative of the American people, elected by the people and responsible only to them." "The Constitution," vol Holst argued, "knows nothing of a President as . . . a direct representative of the American people . . . The only forum before which it cites the President to account for his political acts is the Senate, when the representatives have preferred an impeachment charge against him . . . The Constitution does not know the people at all as Jackson uses the term." It was von Holst's contention that the Jacksonian assertion of the President's right to appeal directly to the nation, by-passing the people's elected representatives in Congress, would result in the creation of an "arbitrary state."[23]

His repudiation of specific Jacksonian policies was generally based upon legal or constitutional grounds. His writings display little interest in economic or social history. Though von Holst, almost alone of the historians of his generation, wrote an unqualified defense of Nicholas Biddle and the Second Bank of the United States, even on this essentially economic issue his case rested primarily on legalistic considerations. Though in one passage he held Jackson responsible for the "frightful disturbances which the economic life of the country experienced" during the last years of his "arbitrary rule," he deemed the Democratic President's banking policies reprehensible primarily because of their alleged violations of the constitutional limitations of executive power Thus, Jackson's use of the veto was found to be "contrary to the spirit of the Constitution" despite the constitutional provisions which granted the President that power. His withholding of the federal funds formerly deposited with the Bank was, in van Holst's view, subversive of the guarantees of the sanctity of contracts embodied in the Constitution. His dismissal of cabinet members without the consent of the Senate was also held to be subversive of the Consti-

---

of von Holst as an historian may be found in Eric Goldman, "Hermann Eduard von Holst, Plumed Knight of American Historiography,"*Mississippi Valley Historical Review*, XXIII, 511-32. See also Charles R. Wilson, "Hermann Eduard von Holst," *Jernegan Essays*, pp. 60-83; Kraus, pp. 192-98; Wish, pp. 210-13.

23. *Constitutional History*, II, 30, 74-79. Indicative of von Holst's commitment to Whig constitutional theories concerning the power of the presidency

tution. Even Jackson's submission of a written paper to his cabinet was regarded as proof of Old Hickory's profound contempt for proper constitutional procedure. If Jackson's pretensions were upheld, von Holst warned ominously, "then the republic will be turned over, bound hand and foot, to one man."[24]

Von holst regarded Jackson's election as the triumph of the mob spirit in American government. In comparing Andrew Jackson to the first President of the United States, he wrote: "Washington was called the embodiment of the best traits of the American national character, but Jackson was the embodiment of all its typical traits. . . . In spite of the frightful influence . . . which he exercised during the eight years of his presidency, he neither pointed out nor opened new ways to his people by the superiority of his mind, but only dragged them more rapidly onwards on the road they had long been travelling, by the demonical power of his will. The supporters of his policy were the instincts of the masses, the sum and substance of it, the satisfaction of those instincts." He argued that Jacksonian rule, by reducing politics to the lowest common denominator and eliminating the role of creative, inspired leadership, had led to "the stagnation of the public spirit" and to the "shallowing, materializing and demoralizing . . . of American democracy." The German historian characterized the tone of Washington society on the eve of Old Hickory's inauguration thus: "The capital of the Union presented a revolting picture. Flattery, servility, espionage, tale bearing and intrigue thrived as they scarcely ever had in the most infamous European courts of the seventeenth and eighteenth centuries, only the court varnish was wanting. Jackson, when not in a towering rage, possessed an unstudied dignity which impressed the masses; but, through the general political pressure of Washington, there ran a streak of genuine brutality." In common with most of the historians of his generation, Hermann von Holst concluded that the Jacksonians had degraded the American Republic.[25]

---

is his remark that "there is no reason, even today, why the warning [concerning Jackson's claims of executive power] which Clay and Webster addressed to the people should be scoffed at." II, 67.

24. *Ibid.*, II, 44-50, 54-68. Few historians of the Constitution today would accept many of von Holst's interpretations of the constitutional issues of the Jackson era. Von Holst's *Constitutional History* was actually much more a history of the slavery controversy than a history of the evolution of the American Constitution.   25. *Ibid.*, II, 24-26, 30-31.

The biographical writing of the Gilded Age reflected this scholarly repudiation of Jacksonian Democracy. John T. Morse, editor of the highly popular *American Statesman* series, expressed the spirit if not the candor of many biographers when he exclaimed to Henry Cabot Lodge: "Let the Jeffersonian and Jacksonian beware! I will poison the popular mind!!" Morse's biography of John Quincy Adams found Jackson "the representative hero of the ignorant masses." Henry Cabot Lodge, in his *Daniel Webster,* concurred, finding Old Hickory's presidential policies the product of "crass ignorance." Henry Adams' *Life of Albert Gallatin* found in the Jacksonian era the beginning of that degeneration of the Republic which he later lamented at greater length in the classic *Education of Henry Adams.* Theodore Roosevelt, though celebrating many of the virtues of the hardy frontiersman in his *Thomas Hart Benton,* deplored the "narrow mind and bitter prejudices" of the first Western president. "Jackson's election," he wrote "is proof that the people are not always right." Carl Schurz's *Life of Henry Clay* charged that "Andrew Jackson violently interrupted good constitutional traditions, and infused into the body politic a spirit of lawlessness which lived after him, and of which the demoralizing influence is felt to this day." Professor Andrew McLaughlin of the University of Michigan, the biographer of Lewis Cass, found Jackson "the conduit pipe through which flowed into the field of national administration a tide of political proscription, intrigue, and legerdemain." Thornton K. Lothrop, in his *Life of William Henry Seward,* wrote that Old Hickory "made war, without regard to constitutional or legal principles or limitations, upon any policy he disbelieved in, or which was supported by the men who withstood his imperious will."[26]

26. Merrill D. Peterson, *The Jefferson Image in the American Mind* (New York, 1960), p. 224; Morse, *John Quincy Adams* (Boston, 1882), pp. 163-218, 225-52; Adams, *The Life of Albert Gallatin* (Philadelphia, 1879), pp. 496-97, 635-37; Lodge, *Daniel Webster* (Boston, 1883), pp. 116, 123; Roosevelt, *Thomas Hart Benton* (Boston, 1886), pp. 19, 22, 33-38, 73-74, 83, 86, 137-39; Schurz, *The Life of Henry Clay* (2 vols., Boston, 1887), II, 107-11; McLaughlin, *Lewis Cass* (Boston, 1891), pp. 2, 137, 145; Lothrop, *The Life of William Henry Seward* (Boston, 1896), p. 20. In common with the historians of the Jacksonian era, Gilded Age biographers frequently approved of specific Jacksonian policies but seldom regarded the Jacksonian influence in American political development as anything except a catastrophe. Of the volumes of the *American Statesmen* series, only Edward Shepard's *Martin Van Buren* (published in 1899 and treated later in the chapter) was basically sympathetic to the Jacksonian movement.

Specialized scholarly studies generally echoed the prevalent conviction that the Jacksonian influence in American politics was a highly pernicious one. Edward Stanwood, in his study of the American presidency, criticized Jackson's "dictatorial tone toward Congress" and castigated his occasional "illegal abuse" of presidential power. Professor Albert S. Bolles of the University of Pennsylvania, in his *Financial History of the United States,* deplored Jackson's "ignorance of sound economics" and held the Jacksonians responsible for the monetary instability of the late 1830's One exception to this predominantly anti-Jacksonian scholarship was Richard T. Ely's *The Labor Movement in America.* Professor Ely of the University of Wisconsin rejected the dominant view of the Jacksonians as corrupters of the Republic. Rather, he argued that the Jacksonian movement was a political expression of the demand of common people of America for social justice. "The Democratic party from 1829 to 1841," Ely wrote, "was more truly a workingmen's party than has been the case with any other great party in our history." In the farmer-labor alliance forged by the Jacksonian movement, Ely found a progressive force later betrayed by both major parties. Though Ely's treatment of the Jacksonian years was, in a sense, the forerunner of a major school of interpretation destined to gain wide support several decades later, it originally attracted almost no favorable consideration. Though other Gilded Age scholars suggested that the Jacksonian movement provided an expression of the class animosities and tensions of the 1830's, they regarded the use of a class appeal by the Jacksonians as further reason for the condemnation of the Jacksonian influence in American life. Their narratives frequently castigated the Jacksonian incitement of the "poor against the rich." Their view of the Jacksonian era, not Richard T. Ely's, shaped the late nineteenth-century image of Jacksonian Democracy.[27]

However, during the 1890's, a decade of political unrest and intellectual ferment, several scholars joined Ely in expressing profound dissatisfaction with the customary historical treatment of the Jacksonian movement. Charles H. Peck, author of the *Jacksonian Epoch,* lamented that the chroniclers of the American past were generally men "under the sway of the Whiggish culture of

27. Stanwood, *A History of the Presidency* (Boston, 1888), pp. 124-79; Bolles, *The Financial History of the United States* (New York, 1883), pp. 317-58; Ely, *The Labor Movement in America* (New York, 1886), pp. 42-43.

18

the country." Edward M. Shepard, biographer of Martin Van Buren, added that most nineteenth-century historians of the Jackson era were totally devoid of sympathy for the "true vitality" of the democratic experiment. The most effective and influential demand for a reappraisal of Jacksonian Democracy, however, came from a young University of Wisconsin professor, Frederick Jackson Turner.[28]

The presentation, at the 1893 convention of the American Historical Association, of Turner's paper, "The Significance of the Frontier in American History," opened a new era in American historiography. Taking issue with the widely accepted "Teutonic Germ" hypothesis of American development, Turner argued that the frontier experience, not our European background, provided the key to the unique and distinctive nature of the nation's basic institutions. Demanding that the West be given some of the attention previously lavished almost exclusively upon Anglo-Saxon heritage, Turner called for a revision of the traditional interpretation of the American past. "The peculiarity of American institutions," he wrote, "is the fact that they have been compelled to adapt themselves to the changes of an expanding people—to the

28. Shepard, *Martin Van Buren* (Boston, 1899) pp. v, 3, 6, 9-12; Donald A. Roberts, "Edward Morse Shepard," *The Dictionary of American Biography*, eds. Allen Johnson and Dumas Malone (New York, 1935), XXVII, 72-73; *The Jacksonian Epoch* (New York, 1899), p. 328. Limitation of space precludes a critical evaluation of the validity of Turner's frontier thesis, which has been subjected to increasing criticism in recent years. See George Rogers Taylor, ed., *The Turner Thesis Concerning the Role of the Frontier in American History* (Boston, 1958); Lee Benson, *Turner and Beard* (Glencoe, Ill., 1960); Avery Craven, "Frederick Jackson Turner," *Jernegan Essays*, pp. 252-70; Gene M. Gressley, "The Turner Thesis, A Problem in Historiography," *Agricultural History*, XXXII, 226-40; Frederic L. Paxson, "A Generation of the Frontier Hypothesis, 1893-1932," *Pacific Historical Review*, II, 34-51; Fulmer Mood, "The Development of Frederick Jackson Turner as a Historical Thinker," *Publications of the Colonial Society of Massachusetts*, XXXIV, 283-352; George Wilson Pierson, "The Frontier and American Institutions: A Criticism of the Turner Theory," *New England Quarterly*, XV, 224-55; "The Frontier and Frontiersmen of Turner's Essay," *Pennsylvania Magazine of History and Biography*, LXIV, 449-78; Benjamin F. Wright, Jr., "American Democracy and the Frontier," *Yale Review*, XX, 349-65; Murray Kane, "Some Considerations of the Frontier Concept of Frederick Jackson Turner," *Mississippi Valley Historical Review*, XXVII, 379-400; Merle Curti, "The Section and the Frontier in American History: The Methodological Concepts of Frederick Jackson Turner," *Methods in Social Science*, ed. Stuart A. Rice (Chicago, 1931), pp. 353-67; Richard Hofstadter, "Turner and the Frontier Myth," *American Scholar*, XVIII, 433-43; Wilbur Jacobs, "Frederick Jackson Turner," *The American West*, I, 32-35, 78-79; Kraus, pp. 278-86; Wish, pp. 181-208.

change involved in crossing a continent, in winning a wilderness, . . . The true point of view in the history of this nation is not the Atlantic coast, it is the Great West . . . Too exclusive attention has been paid by institutional students to Germanic origins, too little to American factors." The nation's democratic heritage, Turner argued, was "fundamentally the outcome of the experiences of the American people in dealing with the West."[29]

Turner attributed some of the noblest aspects of the American character to the frontier influence. "Western democracy," he wrote in 1903, "has been from the very time of its birth idealistic." The unparalleled opportunities of the frontier promoted both individualism and egalitarianism. These Western traits, he argued, contributed decisively to American political evolution. "The frontier states that came into the Union in the first quarter of a century of its existence came in with democratic suffrage provisions, and had reactive effects of the highest importance upon the older states." Democracy, Turner concluded, emerged "stark, strong and full of life from the American forest."[30]

29. "The Significance of the Frontier in American History," Taylor, pp. 1-18. The advocates of the "Teutonic Germ" hypothesis argued that the origins of American institutions were to be found in the tribal customs of primitive teutonic peoples. Transplanted to England by the Anglo-Saxons, these "germs" presumably underwent a slow process of evolution which culminated in maturity after their transfer to the Atlantic seaboard of the United States. Social evolution, in their view, passed through logical, preordained stages of development that could not be altered or accelerated without incurring the most disastrous of consequences. This determinism of course offered no consolation to social reformers who aspired to reshape society in the name of "social justice." It reassured those who believed in stability, permanence, and law, just as it implicitly condemned those who would set "class against class." Though no effort was made to apply the "Teutonic Germ" hypothesis to the Jackson era as such, an excellent example of the application of this theory may be found in Herbert Baxter Adams, "Germanic Origins of New England Towns," *The Johns Hopkins University Studies in Historical and Political Science* (Baltimore, 1883), I, 5-38. Turner did not completely reject Adams' view of social evolution. He held that the thesis was valid as far as it went, but argued that the Western environment, the challenge of the frontier, significantly altered the European heritage. An excellent analysis of Turner's relationship to the "Teutonic Germ" hypothesis is provided in John H. Randall, Jr. and George Haines, IV, "Controlling Assumptions in the Practice of American Historians," *Theory and Practice in Historical Study: A Report of the Committee on Historiography*, Social Science Research Council Bulletin No. 54 (New York, 1946), pp. 17-52.

30. "Significance of the Frontier," *The Frontier in American History* (New York, 1920), pp. 1-2, 14-15, 29. Despite his enthusiastic celebration of the virtues of Western Democracy, Turner shared some of Sumner's misgivings concerning certain aspects of Western life. He deplored the "evil element" of the frontier,

By implication, Turner's frontier thesis challenged the Gilded Age interpretation of the Jacksonian era. Though earlier nineteenth-century scholars had occasionally referred to Jacksonian Democracy as an expression of the Western frontier, they had found little reason to celebrate the triumph of the Western spirit in American politics. But if the West was indeed the birthplace of all that was uniquely American in our heritage, then Andrew Jackson, greatest of the frontiersmen, and those who followed his leadership, could no longer be dismissed simply as backwoods barbarians or condemned out of hand as corrupters of the Republic.

In his 1893 essay, Turner hailed Jackson as the herald of "democracy as an effective force" and proclaimed the Jacksonian movement "the triumph of the frontier." Ten years later, he wrote of Jackson as "the very personification [of the frontier Democracy] . . . free from the influence of European ideas and institutions" and lauded those "men of the Western World [who] with a grim energy and self-reliance began to build up a society free from the dominance of ancient forms." Turner made little effort to disguise his warm affection and admiration for Old Hickory, "that fierce Tennessee spirit who broke down the traditions of conservative rule, swept away the privacies and privileges of officialdom, and, like a Gothic leader, opened the temple of the nation to the populace."[31]

Turner regarded the Jackson movement as a dynamic, invigorating, nationalizing force in American political life. He did not share that aversion to the "turbulence" and "vulgarity" of the Jacksonian Democracy commonly expressed by the older historians of his day. Though condemning the spoils-system politics of his own generation, Turner partially defended the Jacksonian use of "rotation in office" on the grounds that "national government in

---

which bred "lax business honor, inflated paper currency, and wildcat banking." Thinking perhaps of the Populist movement of his own day, which he rejected, Turner acknowledged that frontier individualism at times could exert a pernicious influence in American life. He deplored that "laxity in regard to government affairs which has rendered possible the spoils system and all the manifest evils that follow from the lack of a highly developed civic spirit." But these aspects of Western life appeared to Turner mere minor blemishes when weighed against the West's great contribution to the nation, Democracy and Opportunity, pp. 14-15.

31. *Ibid.*, p. 15; "Contributions of the West to American Democracy," Taylor, pp. 24-25, 32.

that period was no complex and well adjusted machine . . . the evils of the system were long in making themselves fully apparent." In Jackson's generation, he argued, the spoils system "furnished the training in the actual conduct of political affairs which every American claimed as his birthright." Indeed, all aspects of Jackson's administration—the attack upon the Bank, the President's disregard for the niceties of constitutional law, repression of nullification, as well as the spoils system—appeared to Turner as a reflection of the rugged democracy of the frontier, with its intense and wholesome dislike for "ancient forms."[32]

In his later writings, Turner placed primary emphasis upon the role played by sectional conflict in shaping the politics of the Jackson era. In his interpretation, the agrarian states of the West, bastions of Jacksonian Democracy, brought into national life the exuberant, optimistic egalitarianism of the frontier. The manufacturing East and the slaveholding South Atlantic, on the other hand, acted as conservative breaks on the progress of democracy. The election of Jackson, Turner declared, "meant that an agricultural society, strongest in the regions of rural isolation rather than in the areas of greater density of population and of greater wealth, had triumphed over the conservative industrial and manufacturing society of the New England type. It meant that new, expansive democracy, emphasizing human rights and individualism, as against the old established order which emphasized vested rights and corporate action, had come into control." Turner argued that, despite its temporary alliance with the planter interests of the South in 1828, the Jacksonian movement essentially had as little in common with the deep-seated conservatism of the spokesman of the slavocracy as with the emergent eastern industrial interests. The egalitarian ideals of the West, as embodied in Andrew Jackson, "the personification of Western wishes and Western will" were thus in conflict with the entire Eastern seaboard. The great democratizing mission of the Jacksonians, in Turner's analysis, had its origins almost exclusively in the hardy democracy of the frontier.[33]

32. Taylor, p. 25. Though Turner stressed the role of frontier democracy in giving impetus and direction to the Jacksonian crusade for popular rule, he also wrote, in an essay published in 1905, that during Jackson's administration "the labor population of the cities began to assert its power and its determination to share in government." He did not develop this theme, which remained largely ignored for several decades. *The Frontier in American History*, p. 24.

33. *The United States, 1830-1850* (New York, 1935), pp. 36, 381, 383-84, 386.

Turner's interpretation of Jacksonian Democracy as the political expression of frontier nationalism and egalitarianism was echoed in Woodrow Wilson's *Division and Reunion*, which appeared in print several months before Turner's memorable address to the American Historical Association. Michael Kraus, in his history of American historiography, reports that "Wilson unreservedly acknowledged Turner's influence; the two were close friends and talked at length about the significance of the frontier: 'All I ever wrote on the subject came from him,' Wilson said on one occasion." Of Andrew Jackson, Wilson wrote: "He impersonated the agencies that were to nationalize the government. Those agencies may be summed up in two words, 'the West.'" A romantic nationalist of Southern antecedents, Wilson found in the Jacksonian movement a healthy, dynamically nationalistic democracy which transcended the barriers of sectional prejudice and promised to fuse the nation into a united whole. It accorded well with his own vision of an American nationalism grounded in the highest democratic idealism.[34]

Unlike Turner, however, Wilson was highly critical of some of the public policies championed by the Jacksonian party. Though he shared much of the Jacksonian aversion to the Bank of the United States and warned against the perils of leaving "so great, so dominating a financial power in the hands of a giant private corporation," he argued that the Bank had performed a useful function in restraining the note issues of local banks. Warning of the "follies and disasters of unregulated banking," Wilson concluded that the Jacksonians had acted "with an ignorant and almost brutal disregard of the damage that would thereby be done to the delicate fabric of commercial credit." He regarded Jacksonian political techniques, particularly the use of the "spoils system" as a device of party management, "both demoralizing and corrupt." But though Wilson found that the Jacksonians "racked the nicely adjusted frame of government almost to the point of breaking," he nonetheless regarded the Jacksonian influence on American political development a positive and creative one representing "forces of health, hasty because young, possessing the sound but unsensitive

---

In his later writings, Turner also placed somewhat more emphasis upon class antagonisms as a factor in Jacksonian politics. P. 117.

34. *Division and Reunion* (New York, 1893), pp. 24-25; Kraus, p. 216.

conscience which belongs to those who are always confident in action."[35]

A less sympathetic interpretation of the Western influence in the politics of the Jackson era was advanced by John W. Burgess in his study of *The Middle Period*. In dealing with the origins of Jacksonian Democracy, Burgess wrote: "The Western division [of the Jacksonian party] alone was a real democracy. . . . It was the settlement of the country west of the Alleghenies which first created social conditions in harmony with [the democratic] theory." Burgess, however, did not share the enthusiasm for Western Democracy harbored by Turner and Wilson. He followed Sumner in denouncing the "political and social radicalism" of the West and, without defining the term, hinted that Jackson's economic policies smacked of "socialism." A critic of mass democracy, Burgess lamented the passage of government by "the qualified and the able." Indeed, as an intensely conservative Hamiltonian nationalist, Burgess found little to praise in Andrew Jackson or the movement he led. Differing sharply with Turner and Wilson, he declared, disapprovingly, that the election of Jackson in 1828 represented the triumph of a "state rights democracy" hostile to Old Hickory's own nationalistic proclivities. Burgess did, however, approve of Jackson's vigorous use of presidential power, characterizing the frontier general as the "noblest Roman of them all." In that respect, his interpretation of the Jackson era was rather unlike the customary Gilded Age denunciations of "Jacksonian despotism."[36]

In the late 1890's two lesser known Jacksonian scholars, Edward M. Shepard and Charles H. Peck, sought to refute the argument advanced by Burgess and a score of earlier writers that Jacksonian radicalism imperiled the nation's basic institutions. Shepard, a New York lawyer and amateur politician, argued in *Martin Van Buren* that the Jacksonians were actually the true conservatives of their day. Unlike most historians before and since, Shepard did not re-

35. Wilson, pp. 25, 29-34, 69-92. A more detailed statement of Wilson's interpretation of the Jackson era may be found in his *History of the American People* (New York, 1902), IV, 1-144. On Wilson as an historian, see M. L. Daniel, "Woodrow Wilson: Historian," *Mississippi Valley Historical Review*, XXI, 361-74; Louis M. Sears, "Woodrow Wilson," *Jernegan Essays*, pp. 102-21; Kraus, 213-17; Wish, p. 185.

36. *The Middle Period* (New York, 1897), pp. 134-36, 144, 161-65, 193-95, 207-9. Burgess does not mention Turner in his *Middle Period*, but does cite both Sumner and Wilson.

24

gard 1828 as a new departure in American development. The Jacksonian movement, in his view, was pledged to protect the status quo—limited government, states rights, and respect for the Constitution—from those who hoped to establish a revolutionary centralist, paternalistic regime. Shepard, a conservative Democrat who followed Grover Cleveland out of the party in 1896 in protest against Bryan's "radicalism," argued that the true conservatism consisted in jealously maintaining strict limitations on the power of the federal government. Jackson's opponents, he submitted, sought to employ federal internal improvements, a high protective tariff, and a nationally chartered bank as devices to "enormously and radically [change] our system of government." The Jacksonians, in Shepard's analysis, stood in stalwart opposition to the increasingly persistent and subversive demand that government "do something for individuals."[37]

A similar interpretation of the party battles of the Jackson era was advanced in Peck's *Jacksonian Epoch*. Peck argued that the Jacksonians rode to power on the tide of a "popular revolt" which demanded the restoration of the true principle of republican government, "non-interference with popular rights." Deeply influenced by the Social Darwinist philosophy which helped shape many earlier accounts of the Jacksonian era, Peck deplored the American System as a "departure from the law of natural selection." Unlike earlier scholars, he found in the Jacksonian movement no tendencies dangerous to the strictest laissez-faire orthodoxy. He lauded the followers of Old Hickory as faithful disciples of the "true theory" of democratic government and praised even the spoils system as a democratizing device designed to assure popular control over office holders. Peck's interpretation of the "true theory" of government, however, was grounded in principles no good Social Darwinist could question: laissez faire, no government aid to special interests, and free trade. Despite his Jacksonian partisanship, Peck, like Shepard, differed with William Graham Sumner only in his confidence that popular sovereignty would assure the preservation of those principles.[38]

37. Pp. v, 6, 9-12, 98, 102-3, 119-123, 153-56, 178-79. An interesting contrast to Shepard's efforts to enlist the Jacksonians on the side of Grover Cleveland is provided in *The Life and Times of Andrew Jackson* (Thomson, Ga., 1912) written by the Georgia Populist Tom Watson.
38. Pp. 125, 144, 180-235.

Though nineteenth-century scholars, with a few exceptions, were generally agreed in castigating Jacksonian Democracy as a corrupt, demoralizing force in national politics, by 1900 at least five divergent interpretations of the meaning and significance of the movement could be found in the historiography of the Jackson era. In one version represented by Parton, Tucker, Schouler, and many others, the Jacksonians were portrayed as traitors to the Jeffersonian heritage. These writers contended that the despotic abuses of presidential power, the political corruption, and the demagogic appeals to mass prejudice presumably associated with the Jacksonian movement constituted the very antithesis of the statesmanlike democratic-republicanism of Jefferson and the founders of the Democratic party. Another interpretation, advanced by Sumner and von Holst, concurred in deploring Jacksonian radicalism, but found the roots of the Jacksonian "degradation of the Republic" in the very Jeffersonian principles lauded by Parton and his followers. These conservatives called for strict constitutional restraints upon the majority will to guarantee social stability and to assure respect for the rights of property. In the 1880's, a lone scholar, Richard T. Ely, argued that the Jacksonian appeal to the masses constituted, not irresponsible demagogery, but true concern for social justice. In the 1880's, Turner and Wilson sought to defend Jacksonian Democracy as an expression of the creative and wholesome nationalistic democracy of the frontier, while Shepard and Peck endeavored to cast the Jacksonians in the role of popular champions of the conservative principles of states' rights and laissez faire.

Though the vigorous polemical tone which characterized their writings strikes the modern reader as quaint and even vaguely improper, the interpretations of the Jacksonian movement first advanced by nineteenth-century writers have frequently reappeared, usually in more refined and sophisticated form, in the Jacksonian historiography of later decades. Their role in shaping the historian's concept of Jacksonian Democracy should not be minimized.

2. JACKSONIAN
HISTORIOGRAPHY, 1900-1945

Both the Gilded Age portrayal of the Jacksonian movement as a destructive, degrading expression of the mob spirit in politics and Frederick Jackson Turner's new image of the Jacksonians as rugged but idealistic champions of the vital, hardy democracy of the American West influenced early twentieth-century Jacksonian historiography. But though the prodemocratic interpretation of the Jacksonian movement was never accorded the uncritical acceptance once enjoyed by the conservative, anti-Jacksonian version, most of the historians of Turner's generation tended to portray Jacksonian Democracy as the fulfillment, rather than the betrayal, of the nation's political tradition. Some, indeed, were as uncritical in their glorification of the Jeffersonian-Jacksonian heritage as their nineteenth-century counterparts had been in their interpretation of the Jacksonian as spoilsman and demagogue.

John Bach McMaster's treatment of the Jacksonian era in his massive *History of the People of the United States* reflected both the new spirit of Jacksonian partisanship and the older aversion to Jacksonian Democracy. McMaster, a professor of American history at the University of Pennsylvania, wrote of the movement to extend popular control of government as "a struggle between the rights of property and the rights of man." His avowed sympathies were on the side of the rights of man. Describing Andrew Jackson as "a man of the people, . . . devoted to their interests and knowing their wants," he hailed Old Hickory's election as a "triumph of Democracy." None of the doubt concerning the wisdom of majority rule that permeated the writings of Sumner and von Holst can be found in McMaster's interpretation of the American past. On the contrary, as his biographer remarks, "No American historian, not even Bancroft, has ever glorified the people more."[1]

McMaster, like Turner, spoke of Andrew Jackson as the representative hero of the American West. Though he placed somewhat

1. *History of the People of the United States* (New York, 1883-1912), V, 55-58, 383-85, 488; Eric Goldman, *John Bach McMaster* (Philadelphia, 1943), p. 142. On McMaster as an historian see also William T. Hutchinson, "John Bach McMaster," *Jernegan Essays*, pp. 122-43; Kraus, 218-25; Wish, pp. 131-57.

less emphasis upon the Western influence in Jacksonian politics, he followed Turner in arguing that the Jacksonian employment of the spoils system in national administration, so grave a sin against the Republic in the eyes of earlier historians, was in fact a necessary weapon in the battle for popular rule. He justified its use as essential in shattering the rule of the old aristocracy "which had used the federal patronage to carry elections and the federal treasury to reward its followers." Concerning Jackson's removal policy, McMaster added: "As we look back on those days, the wonder is, not that so many were turned out of office, but that so many were suffered to remain."[2]

Despite his praise for the Jacksonian democratization of national government, it does not follow, as some commentators have erroneously concluded, that McMaster was a thoroughly uncritical partisan of the Jacksonian movement. Actually, his narrative provided one of the severest castigations of Jacksonian economic policies ever written. His fervid belief in the principle of popular rule notwithstanding, McMaster's treatment of the Jacksonian assault on the Bank of the United States expressed profound disgust with the blind prejudices of the masses who sustained the Jacksonian cause. Dismissing the charges against the Bank as the product of sheer ignorance and demagogery, he remarked, somewhat derisively, "Hundreds of thousands of voters had never seen one of its branches nor one of its notes, nor ever had a cent on deposit in its vaults." He argued that the misinformed financial blunderings of Old Hickory and his cohorts had created inestimable suffering for the common people of the land, whose interests they professed to defend. Through their folly, he wrote, "the whole system of exchange was suddenly and unexpectedly thrown into confusion." McMaster also condemned the inflationary monetary schemes espoused by many Jacksonians as both "vicious" and "absurd." Despite his praise for Andrew Jackson as a "man of the people," McMaster belittled Old Hickory's presidential leadership and deplored his inadequate knowledge of "principles of government." In some passages, he echoed earlier conservative historians in writing of the Jacksonian period as the "era of mob rule."[3]

Though McMaster lauded both "Democracy" and "the rule of the people" throughout his *History of the People of the United*

2. McMaster, V. 518-22.   3. *Ibid*, VI, 55, 186, 192.

States, he often used those words as mere cabalistic phrases. He sometimes accepted quite uncritically partisan propaganda hostile to the popular political movements of the past. The leading authority on Jeffersonian historiography has remarked of his treatment of the Sage of Monticello: "Behind the imposing facade of the eight volumes of the *History,* the historian announced opinions which had little foundation other than Federalist prejudice." With some reservations, the same observation could be made of his evaluation of Andrew Jackson's presidency. McMaster was actually almost as conservative as the anti-Jacksonian writers of the previous generation. His pronounced sympathy for democracy as a political movement notwithstanding, McMaster's personal views on most contemporary political issues—free silver, Populism, economic reform—tended to be quite hostile to social change. Though Mc-Master was one of the first scholars to investigate the labor movement of the Jacksonian era and sympathized with the labor grievances of the 1830's, he opposed the labor militancy of his own day. He expressed the hope that his writings would be "full of instruction" to all radical reformers. Through an appreciation of the past, McMaster declared, they might come to abandon their Utopian schemes and accept the great social gains which the gradual evolution of popular rule in America had already made possible. McMaster's *History,* remarked Eric Goldman, "voted for Mc-Kinley."[4]

Two monographs published in the early 1900's one by Professor Ralph C. H. Catterall of the University of Chicago and the other by Carl Russell Fish, professor of American History at the University of Wisconsin, exerted a profound influence upon subsequent scholarly studies of the Jacksonian era. *The Second Bank of the United States,* by Catterall, offered impressive, thoroughly documented support to those who deplored the Jacksonian ignorance of sound economics. Catterall, the first scholar to gain access to Nicholas Biddle's personal papers, concluded, after a careful study of the Second Bank's activities, that Biddle's institu-

---

4. *Ibid.,* II, 616-17; Peterson, p. 279; Goldman, p. 143. Michael Kraus has noted rather cogently that McMaster, "in his thinking and in his writing . . . generally identified the 'people' with the middle class." McMaster's moderate sympathy for the labor movements of the past is best expressed in his *The Acquisition of Political, Social and Industrial Rights of Man in America* (Cleveland, 1903). His essential conservatism is given further expression in his laudatory *Daniel Webster* (New York, 1902).

tion, by controlling and regulating state chartered banks of issue and by providing sound banking facilities to the federal government, had performed an indispensible public service. "The old bank," he wrote, "in its services to the government was far superior to any other banking system known in this country." He deplored the destruction of the Bank by misinformed politicians who, though generally sincere in their beliefs, lacked real understanding of financial matters. He expressed regret that the political influence of "enlightened business men" in politics "has always been inconsiderable, partly because they are not interested in politics, partly because they are themselves the objects of suspicion to the democratic masses." He declared that it was "obvious that Jackson and his supporters committed an offense against the nation when they destroyed the Bank. The magnitude and enormity of that offense can only faintly be realized, but one is certainly justified in saying that few greater enormities are chargeable to politicians than the destruction of the Bank of the United States."[5]

Despite that conclusion, however, Catterall was not entirely uncritical of the Second Bank. Though he found that the Jacksonian indictment of the Bank as a corrupt, unsound, and dangerous institution was essentially without foundation at the time, Catterall charged that Biddle in 1833 and 1834 sought to coerce the nation into supporting recharter by plunging the economy into a severe crisis through restrictions of credit not justified by the Bank's actual economic condition. "The president and company of the Bank," he wrote, "were in fact, not only frightened by Jackson's attack, but angry; not merely angry, but vindictive, and vindictive with calculation. They hoped to force a recharter or at least a restoration of the deposits, by exercising a monetary pressure upon

5. *The Second Bank of the United States* (Chicago, 1903), pp. 132-358, 453-77. Other economic historians generally agreed with Catterall's findings. Prior to the publication of *The Second Bank*, a former comptroller of the currency, John Jay Knox, in his *History of Banking in the United States* (New York, 1900), deplored the Jacksonian destruction of Biddle's institution as a serious blow against financial stability. Knox did not, however, fully appreciate the nature of the bank's stabilization operations. Knox, pp. 51-80. Davis R. Dewey's enormously popular *Financial History of the United States* (New York, 1902) resembled Knox in its treatment of the Jacksonian controversy with the Bank. Dewey, pp. 197-252. Dewey provided a more detailed study of Biddle's institution in a study undertaken for the National Monetary Fund, *The Second United States Bank* (Washington, 1910). Some years later, a valuable survey of Jacksonian economic ideas was provided in M. G. Madeleine, *Monetary and Banking Theories of Jacksonian Democracy* (Philadelphia, 1943).

the country." He found Biddle's attitude "viciously unjust, for it struck at the guilty by inflicting penalties upon the innocent, and the innocent were men and women who were, to a considerable number, friends and partisans of the Bank." The tragic failure of the efforts to recharter the Second Bank were, in Catterall's judgment, the result not only of Jackson's ignorant malice and the uninformed prejudices of his followers, but also of Biddle's own arrogance, ruthlessness, and lack of political tact. Later historians who rejected Catterall's defense of the Bank often cited his analysis of Biddle's conduct during the Bank war to support their own pro-Jacksonian conclusions.[6]

Fish's impressively documented study of *The Civil Service and the Patronage* lent weight to the demands for a revision of the customary interpretation of the Jacksonian spoils system earlier voiced by Turner and McMaster. Fish offered ample statistical evidence to demonstrate that the opponents of Jackson—and those historians who had accepted uncritically their partisan fulminations—had greatly exaggerated the actual number of partisan removals during the Jacksonian years. In sharp contrast to the Gilded Age interpretation of the spoils system as a demoralizing prostitution of the civil service to the corrupt plunderings of venal politicians, Fish also argued that the use of public office as a partisan device was historically essential to the establishment of a responsive, popularly controlled party organization. "If the majority is to mould the policy of the party, if the *demos* is to be kept constantly awake and brought out to vote after the excitement of the hour has passed," he wrote, "it is necessary that the party be organized. . . . Now some men may labor for love and some for glory, but glory comes only to the leaders of the ten thousands—to the very few—it cannot serve as a general inducement and even those who love must live." Contrary to the tacit patrician assumptions of many of the earlier scholars of the Jackson era, Fish argued that "it is an essential idea of democracy that these leaders shall be of the people; they must not be gentlemen of wealth and leisure, but they must—the mass of them at any rate—belong to the class that makes its own living. If, then, they are to devote their time to politics, politics must be made to pay. It is here that the function of the spoils system becomes evident; the civil service becomes the payroll of the party leader; offices are apportioned according to the rank and merit

6. Catterall, pp. 314-31.

of his subordinates, and, if duties are too heavy or new positions are needed, new offices may be created. To apply these facts to America, the spoils system paid for the party organization which enabled the democracy of Pennsylvania to rule after 1800 and which established a 'government of the people' in the United States in 1829."[7]

Fish was by no means insensitive to the abuses which followed the advent of the spoils system. He argued, however, that these abuses had been greatly overemphasized, while the accomplishment of the system had been too often totally ignored. Its use, Fish maintained, was essential to the creation of a true democracy in America. Fish concluded his analysis of the Jacksonian appointment policies with a plea that these policies be viewed in the context of the Jackson era. "The armor in which democracy won its great victories in America and to which it still clings in great part may now seem crude and heavy and inapt to the wearer; but we should not forget that at the time of its introduction it was the very best that had been devised, that by it, for the first time in history, a numerous and very widely scattered people was enabled to direct its whole force to its own advancement, and present appreciation of the evils of the spoils system should not blind us to the fact that in the period of its establishment it served a purpose that could probably have been performed in no other way and was fully worth the cost."[8]

7. *The Civil Service and the Patronage* (New York, 1905), pp. 156-57. However, for a contemporary restatement of the older view of the Jacksonian influence, see Moisie Ostrogorski, *Democracy and the Organization of Political Parties* (2 vols., New York, 1902), II. Fish's findings were confirmed in a later investigation, E. M. Erikkson, "The Federal Civil Service Under President Jackson," *Mississippi Valley Historical Review*, XIII, 517-40. More recently, Leonard D. White's scholarly and authoritative volume, *The Jacksonians, A Study in Administrative History 1829-1861* (New York, 1954), followed Fish in rejecting the dramatic and lurid charges levelled against the Jacksonian spoils system by opposition partisans and Gilded Age scholars, but raised new questions concerning the wisdom of Jacksonian policies. Though the system "had a unique asset, because it enabled many citizens to participate in the business of government," as an administrative device "the patronage system had a fatal defect, because it possessed a double loyalty, one to the executive branch of the government, the other to the political party." White also found that the level of the public service deteriorated under Jackson, but attributed this, not to any special Jacksonian depravity, but rather to "a general decline in business morality." White, pp. 300-43, 420. For an excellent survey of the historiography of the spoils system, to 1939, see Frank Freidel, "Jackson's Political Removals as seen by Historians," *The Historian*, II, 41-52.   8. Fish, pp. 156-57.

William MacDonald's *Jacksonian Democracy*, published as the fifteenth volume of the influential *American Nation* series, gave somewhat qualified support to the new spirit of rebellion against the conservative, anti-Jacksonian tradition in American historiography. MacDonald, a professor of history at Brown University, found many aspects of the Jacksonian movement most unattractive. Though he followed Frederick Jackson Turner in regarding the West as the source of the vigorous egalitarianism of the Jackson era, he was far more critical than Turner of the crudity, prejudice, and lack of culture which, in his judgment, characterized both the frontier and the Jacksonian movement. He found Andrew Jackson a poorly educated, arbitrary frontier chieftain whose demogogic claims to "intuitive knowledge" of the popular will could only be regarded as "dangerous." He deplored Old Hickory's lack of understanding of the economic results of his banking policy. The spoils system MacDonald labelled "obviously unprincipled and demoralizing." Many passages of *Jacksonian Democracy* were highly reminiscent of the judgments of Gilded Age scholars of the Jackson era.[9]

On balance, however, MacDonald found the Jacksonian influence in American politics a wholesome one. Despite his revulsion over the Jacksonian "attack on the civil service," he agreed partially with Fish that the spoils system helped to democratize American government by breaking "the hold of the official class." In spite of his distaste for Jackson's gross ignorance of the principles of money and banking, MacDonald approved of Old Hickory's opposition to the rechartering of the Second Bank of the United States. "His attack upon the Bank was brutal," he wrote, "but the Bank was nevertheless a gigantic monopoly whose abatement was of inestimable benefit to the political and economic life of the country." His aversion to Jackson's "arbitrary" and "high-handed" ways notwithstanding, MacDonald lauded Old Hickory's vigorous use of presidential power, arguing that the nation was thereby saved from congressional despotism. Unlike those historians who had earlier found the Jacksonians guilty of degrading the American political heritage, MacDonald praised their work in reviving "meaningful political distinctions" and lauded their masterful command of the techniques of party organization. He found the greatest Jacksonian contribution to the nation, however, in their

9. *Jacksonian Democracy, 1828-1837* (New York, 1907), pp. 24-30, 42, 53-54, 60, 65-66, 116-31, 178, 221-28.

33

fulfillment of the Jeffersonian promise of popular rule. The Jacksoians, MacDonald concluded, transformed the democratic theory into "what it had never been before in the United States, a working scheme of government."[10]

As the twentieth century progressed, Frederick Jackson Turner's interpretation of Jacksonian Democracy as an expression of the Western spirit won increasing scholarly acceptance. John Spencer Bassett, in his two volume *Life of Andrew Jackson*, the first significant scholarly appraisal of Old Hickory's political career since Sumner's *Andrew Jackson as a Public Man*, declared that the Jacksonian movement represented the triumph of the values of the American West in national politics. Jackson, he wrote, "voiced the thought of the frontier, which happened to be the average thought of the older parts of America . . . his Western ideals were for him the only ideals. They gave him his battle cry, which, when once uttered, found support in the hearts of average Americans everywhere. And this was the secret of the Jacksonian movement." Occasionally, Bassett, like Turner, alluded to the existence of class cleavages in the political parties of the Jackson era. He found, for example, that "the mercantile classes and men of wealth generally" rather consistently opposed the Jacksonian movement. But these class antagonisms, in his analysis, were secondary. The conflict of sections and the dominant influence of the West, to Bassett, constituted the major themes of the Jacksonian era.[11]

10. *Ibid*, 65-66, 171, 184, 228, 236, 282, 303, 307, 315.
11. Bassett, *The Life of Andrew Jackson* (New York, 1935), pp. ix, 421, 489, 622. Bassett's *Jackson* first appeared in 1911; these citations are from a later printing of that edition. Several minor biographies of Old Hickory appeared during the early 1900's: William G. Brown, *Andrew Jackson* (Boston, 1900); Augustus C. Buell, *History of Andrew Jackson* (2 vols., New York, 1904); Cyrus Brady, *The True Andrew Jackson* (Philadelphia, 1906); Arthur Colyar, *Life and Times of Andrew Jackson* (Nashville, 1904). These biographies were all quite superficial. At least one of them, Buell's, was highly unreliable due to the author's unfortunate tendency to fabricate many of his sources. See Milton W. Hamilton, "Augustus C. Buell, Fraudulent Historian," *Pennsylvania Magazine of History and Biography*, LXXX, 478-92. Of more value, as personal portraits of Old Hickory, were two biographies published during the 1920's, Gerald W. Johnson's, *Andrew Jackson: An Epic in Homespun* (New York, 1927) and David Karsner's *Andrew Jackson, The Gentle Savage* (New York, 1929). Among the biographies of Jackson's contemporaries published between 1900 and 1945 were Frederic Bancroft, *The Life of William Seward* (2 vols., New York, 1900); Samuel W. McCall, *Daniel Webster* (Boston, 1902); John Bach McMaster, *Daniel Webster* (New York, 1902); Joseph M. Rogers, *True Henry Clay* (New York, 1902); Howard W. Caldwell, *Henry Clay* (Milwaukee, 1903); Gustavus C. Pinck-

Bassett expressed certain misgivings concerning the political ascendency of the "average man." Though praising the courage, honesty, and vigorous presidential leadership of Andrew Jackson— who, in his judgment, personified both the virtues and the weaknesses of the typical American of his generation—he was rather critical of Old Hickory's alleged narrowness, ignorance, naiveté, and

ney, *Life of John C. Calhoun* (Charleston, 1903); William M. Meigs, *The Life of Thomas Hart Benton* (Philadelphia, 1904); Joseph M. Rogers, *Thomas H. Benton* (Philadelphia, 1905); Everett P. Wheeler, *Daniel Webster, The Expounder of the Constitution* (New York, 1905); Gaillard Hunt, *John C. Calhoun* (Philadelphia, 1908); T. D. Jervey, *Robert Y. Hayne and His Times* (New York, 1909); J. E. D. Shipp, *Giant Days; or, The Life and Times of William H. Crawford* (Americus, Ga., 1909); Thomas H. Clay and Ellis P. Oberholtzer, *Henry Clay* (Philadelphia, 1910); Sidney George Fisher, *True Daniel Webster* (New York, 1911); C. H. Ambler, *Thomas Ritchie* (Richmond, 1913); Frederick A. Ogg, *Daniel Webster* (Philadelphia, 1914); William M. Meigs, *The Life of John Caldwell Calhoun* (2 vols., New York, 1917); E. I. McCormac, *James K. Polk* (Berkeley, 1922); Claude M. Fuess, *The Life of Caleb Cushing* (2 vols., New York, 1923); Allen L. Benson, *Daniel Webster* (New York, 1929); Marquis James, *The Raven: A Biography of Sam Houston* (Indianapolis, 1929); Dennis T. Lynch, *An Epoch and A Man; Martin Van Buren and His Times* (New York, 1929); James Truslow Adams, *The Adams Family* (Boston, 1930); Samuel Hopkins Adams, *The Godlike Daniel* (New York, 1930); Claude M. Fuess, *Daniel Webster* (2 vols., Boston, 1930); J. H. Parks, *John Bell of Tennessee* (Baton Rouge, 1930); Queena Pollack, *Peggy Eaton* (New York, 1931); Bennett Champ Clark, *John Quincy Adams, Old Man Eloquent* (Boston, 1932); Leland Winfield Meyer, *The Life and Times of Colonel Richard M. Johnson of Kentucky* (New York, 1932); William E. Smith, *The Francis Preston Blair Family in Politics* (2 vols., New York, 1933); Linda Rhea, *Hugh Swinton Legaré* (Chapel Hill, 1934); Holmes M. Alexander, *The American Tallyrand; The Career and Contemporaries of Martin Van Buren* (New York, 1935); H. E. Putnam, *Joel Roberts Poinsett* (Washington, 1935); Arthur Styron, *The Cast-Iron Man; John C. Calhoun and American Democracy* (Toronto, 1935); Carl Brent Swisher, *Roger B. Taney* (New York, 1935); G. R. Poage, *Henry Clay and the Whig Party* (Chapel Hill, 1936); C. W. Smith, *Roger B. Taney, Jacksonian Jurist* (Chapel Hill, 1936); A. D. H. Smith, *Old Fuss and Feathers, the Life . . . of Winfield Scott* (New York, 1937); Glyndon G. Van Deusen, *The Life of Henry Clay* (Boston, 1937); Oliver P. Chitwood, *John Tyler* (New York, 1939); Freeman Cleaves, *Old Tippecanoe: William Henry Harrison and his Times* (New York, 1939); John T. Horton, *James Kent: A Study in Conservatism, 1763-1847* (New York, 1939); Arthur M. Schlesinger, Jr., *Orestes A. Brownson* (Boston, 1939); William B. Hatcher, *Edward Livingston; Jeffersonian, Republican and Jacksonian Democrat* (Baton Rouge, 1940); Joseph H. Parks, *Felix Grundy, Champion of Democracy* (Baton Rouge, 1940); Holman Hamilton, *Zachary Taylor* (Indianapolis, 1941). Many of these biographies dealt casually, or not at all, with the political issues of the Jacksonian era. Only a few offered a comprehensive analysis of the Jacksonian movement. As a group, the biographies were less influenced by the new trend towards a sympathetic treatment of the Jacksonian movement than were the authors of the narrative histories and specialized studies of the Jackson era.

35

provincialism. The first Western president, he wrote, was "a man of passion" whose political views "were formed through feeling rather than intellect." He deplored the "superficiality" of Jackson's "ideas of finance" and, with Catterall, deemed Nicholas Biddle's efforts to convince the nation of the need for rechartering the Second Bank of the United States "a task of enlightenment." Of the Jacksonian crusade against the Bank, Bassett wrote: "The courage of the anti-Bank men was admirable, their generalship was excellent; but their methods were not always commendable. Prejudice, ignorance and selfishness abounded rather more than on the other side."[12]

Bassett, however, declared, with obvious approbation, that under Jackson "the tendency to aristocratic institutions in the hands of conservative republicans was replaced by a vigorous and well organized democratic party." Frequently praising the Jacksonians for their genius in political organization, he reluctantly decided that the spoils system, which he regarded as basically pernicious, was but a natural expression of the Jacksonian quest for a truly democratic political order. In summarizing Jackson's personal contribution to that quest, Bassett wrote: "The American who now knows how to estimate the life of the Jacksonian era will take something from the pretensions of his enemies and add something to the virtues hitherto accorded his partisans. Jackson's lack of education, his crude judgments in many affairs, his occasional outbreaks of passion, his habitual hatred of those enemies with whom he had not made friends for party purposes, and his crude ideas of some political policies, all lose some of their infelicity in the face of his brave, frank, masterly leadership of the democratic movement which then established itself in our life."[13]

Even more fervid than Bassett in his basic Jacksonian partisanship was Professor William E. Dodd of the University of Chicago. In his *Expansion and Conflict* Dodd dismissed the foes of Old Hickory as timorous aristocrats who feared the rough ways of plain men and opposed the ideals of equality and popular initiative basic to the American heritage. Portraying Andrew Jackson as the heir and defender of the egalitarian heritage of Thomas Jefferson, he declared that, prior to 1828, "the old Jeffersonian machine, organized as a popular protest against aristocracy and the money

12. Bassett, pp. 408, 431, 483.
13. *Ibid.*, p. 750.

36

power, had itself become aristocratic, and it had ceased to represent the democracy of the United States." Jackson, by rallying the "social classes" which had supported Jefferson in 1800, revitalized the Jeffersonian democratic tradition. With Old Hickory's election, Dodd wrote, "the people had come to power a second time." The party battles of the Jackson era, in Dodd's analysis, emanated from the popular determination to control government, despite the opposition of "strong willed aristocrats" such as Nicholas Biddle who "put little faith in popular elections and plebiscites." In highly partisan terms, Dodd glorified Andrew Jackson as the spokesman of the common man, proclaiming Old Hickory "the second American president who so understood his people he could interpret them and by intuition scent the course the popular mind would take."[14]

Dodd's interpretation of the origins of the Jacksonian movement echoed Frederick Jackson Turner's frontier thesis. He found that the "great West, pulsating with life and vigor, filled with hope for the future, at once democratic and imperialistic," provided "the nucleus of the party of Jackson." Dodd also followed Turner in emphasizing the importance of the sectional conflict during the Jacksonian era. Of ante-bellum American politics, he wrote, "the decisive motive behind the different groups in Congress at every great crisis under discussion was sectional advantage or even sectional aggrandisement." However, Dodd placed somewhat heavier emphasis upon the conflict of "social classes" as a force in Jacksonian politics than had Turner. He found that during the 1830's "the small farmers of the country districts and the artisan classes of the East accepted the leadership of the West and waged relentless war on behalf of the 'Old Hero.'" Indeed, Dodd found economic motives generally decisive in shaping political action, and applying this thesis to the Jackson era, he characterized the Bank war as a struggle to prevent "the subordination of the country to one of its interests" and commented upon the pronounced tendency of the prosperous to gravitate to the Whig camp as that struggle progressed. But though he regarded the conflict of economic interests as the motive force underlying American political life, Dodd conceived of that struggle primarily as one of sections, not classes. Class conflict was the secondary, not the dominant theme, of his interpretation of the Jacksonian era. Essentially, his portrayal of

14. *Expansion and Conflict* (Boston, 1915), pp. 1-4, 9-12, 15, 19, 21, 37, 78.

the Jacksonian movement accorded with the conceptions of Frederick Jackson Turner.[15]

Turner's conceptions were also endorsed, somewhat less enthusiastically, in Frederick Austin Ogg's *The Reign of Andrew Jackson.* Professor Ogg, of the University of Wisconsin, found Turner's uninhibited celebration of Jacksonian frontier democracy in some respects quite uncongenial. Far from rejoicing in the egalitarian upheaval symbolized by Jackson's election, Ogg noted with aversion the "promiscuous multitude" that followed Old Hickory's leadership and included in his summation of the Jacksonian achievement a condemnation of the spoils system as a permanently harmful "debauchery of the civil service," quite reminiscent of the judgments of Gilded Age historians of the Jackson era. He was most critical of Jackson's personal "irascibility, egotism, stubbornness and intolerance of the opinions of others," and found his monetary policies compounded of malice, misinformation, and prejudice. But nonetheless, Ogg perceived in the election of the "untrained, self-willed, passionate frontier soldier" the triumph of "a mighty democratic uprising which was destined before it ran its course to break down oligarchial party organizations, to liberalize state and local governments and to turn the stream of national life into wholly new channels." Ogg followed the revisionists in finding the source of the "democratic uprising" of the Jackson era in the egalitarianism of the Western frontier, in regarding the sectional conflict as the dynamic force behind the party battles of the Jackson era, and in praising Jackson's fervid nationalism and vigorous executive leadership. "In his vindication of executive independence, Jackson broke new ground, crudely enough it is true; yet whatever the merits of his ideas at the moment they reshaped men's conception of the presidency and helped to make that office the power it is today." Ogg concluded his evaluation of Jackson's presidency with praise for Old Hickory's democratic idealism. "He was not a statesman," he wrote, "yet some of the highest qualities of statesmanship were in him. He had a perception of the public will which has rarely been surpassed and in most, if not all, of the great issues of his time he had a grasp of the right side of the question."[16]

15. *Ibid.*, pp. v-vi.
16. *The Reign of Andrew Jackson* in *The Frontier in Politics* ("The Chronicles of America Series," ed. Allen Johnson [New York, 1919]), pp. 114, 235-36.

Carl Russell Fish's pioneering social history of the Jacksonian era, *The Rise of the Common Man*, published twenty-two years after *The Civil Service and the Patronage*, also bore the mark of Turner's influence. Fish declared of the inhabitants of the West whose support elevated Andrew Jackson to the Presidency: "Not by numbers alone . . . but by their crude embodiment of the spirit of the age they prepared to lead the country. Their partial success marks the first case in history of a nation dominated by a frontier population." Fish argued that the Jacksonian influence in American life represented, not merely a general lowering of standards among the higher classes and a consequent triumph of mediocrity, as Gilded Age historians had frequently maintained, but also a simultaneous "levelling upwards," a pervasive improvement in the level and tone of American life. Even so, Fish betrayed a certain uneasiness as to the ultimate implications of the Jacksonian cult of the common man. Contrasting Andrew Jackson and Ralph Waldo Emerson, Fish wrote: "The ultimate tendency of Jackson's view would have been to a dull effort by a satisfied sameness. Equality to Emerson was a reward of striving." Though Fish fully shared the Jacksonians' distaste for elitism and regarded the triumph of Jackson as a praiseworthy triumph of the "people" over the "aristocracy," he was nonetheless clearly relieved that the Jacksonian conception of equality was never fully realized.[17]

Though the Turner theory of the origins of Jacksonian Democracy was accorded widespread scholarly acceptance during the first two decades of the twentieth century, dissenting voices were heard with increasing frequency during the 1920's and 1930's. Turner's eminent Harvard University colleague, Edward Channing, challenged the fundamental premise of the frontier interpretation of Jacksonian Democracy in the fifth volume of his *History of the United States*. Channing contended that Turner had erred in regarding the West as the dominant force in the Jacksonian political alliance. The movement Jackson led, he submitted, was in actuality the expression of the states' rights conservatism of the southern planter interests. "Jackson," Channing wrote, "was really

17. *The Rise of the Common Man* (New York, 1927), pp. ix, xvii, 1, 4, 9, 11, 21, 30-31, 41-42, 45-50, 52, 164, 169, 172. Similar misgivings were expressed in Ralph Barton Perry's *Puritanism and Democracy* (New York, 1944). Alice Felt Tyler's *Freedom's Ferment* (Minneapolis, 1944) provided an excellent study of the humanitarian and utopian movements of the Jacksonian era, an area often underemphasized by Jacksonian scholars.

chosen to the presidency by the solid South, as was quite proper as he was a Southern man, a slaveholder and a cotton planter." The basic sectional conflicts in Jacksonian politics, as Channing saw it, divided the North and the South, not the East and the West. Differing with Turner in regarding the Southwest as an integral part of the "solid South," rather than of the frontier West, Channing contended that Jackson's political success was made possible only by Southern support. "However one manipulates the figures, it would seem that Jackson was raised to the presidency by the over-representation of the South." Though the planters had entered into a tenuous alliance with the emergent radicalism of the Northern urban democracy, that alliance, in Channing's view, was thoroughly dominated by the planter's reactionary viewpoint. Jackson, he argued, "held to the full the southern ideas, balking only at nullification." Only on the question of the "reconstruction of the civil service" did Jackson's ideas conform to the views of "Northern radicalism." Regarding Jackson's views of the American System, states' rights, and strict construction basically those of a Southern conservative, Channing portrayed Old Hickory as a "master politician who successfully harmonized southern agricultural and northern democratic interests" without yielding to the demands of the real democrats of his day. President Jackson, he concluded, "used the powers of his office to restrain rather than to execute." Channing disagreed not only with Turner's analysis of the origins and nature of the Jacksonian movement but also with his sympathetic portrayal of the Jacksonian influence in American political life. An admirer of John Quincy Adams and the political tradition Adams symbolized, Channing deplored the "demagoguery" of Jacksonian electioneering and labelled the inauguration of the spoils system "one of the greatest scandals in our history." A fervid nationalist, he pronounced Old Hickory's followers proponents of the narrowest localism. The Bank war, in his view, "was really part of the never ending struggle between localism and nationalism," a struggle in which the Jacksonians, out of ignorance and malice, championed the antinationalistic position. In Channing's pages, the Jacksonian movement was thus portrayed as a reactionary, not a progressive, force in the nation's political development.[18]

18. *A History of the United States* (New York, 1926), V, 351-52, 368, 375-95, 423, 434-47, 455. On Channing as an historian see Ralph Ray Fahrney, "Edward Channing," *Jernegan Essays*, pp. 294-312; Samuel Eliot Morison, "Ed-

Perhaps the most provocative interpretation of Andrew Jackson's personal role in American politics advanced by the critics of the Turner school was provided by Professor Thomas P. Abernethy of the University of Virginia. Unlike Channing, Abernethy did not challenge the thesis that the Jacksonians came to power as a result of popular democratic upsurge. He did, however, question the tendency of historians to glorify Old Hickory as the folk hero of the frontier democracy. After a careful study of Andrew Jackson's role in Tennessee politics prior to his elevation to the presidency, Abernethy concluded that Old Hickory, for both personal and economic reasons, had tended to support candidates hostile to the rising democratic reform movement in his home state. Jackson, far from being a dedicated champion of the interests of the common man, was in fact, Abernethy argued, a "frontier aristocrat" whose support of various questionable political measures designed to assist speculators betrayed a profound insensitivity to the best interests of the majority. The conversion of Jackson and his immediate followers to the democratic cause, he maintained, was sheer opportunism. Basically, as a man of wealth, Jackson was quite opposed to economic reform movements (such as the relief and debtor stay law schemes of the early 1820's) which might imperil the rights of landed property. He was further quite devoid of any conscious political philosophy or any real commitment to democratic idealism. Of Jackson, Abernethy concluded: "He always believed in making the public serve the ends of the politician. Democracy was good talk with which to win the favor of the people and thereby accomplish ulterior motives. Jackson never really championed the cause of the people, he only invited them to champion his." He added, however, that Jackson "was not consciously hypocritical in this. It was merely the usual way of doing business in those primitive and ingenuous times." Abernethy's skepticism of Old Hickory's democratic idealism was fully shared by Richard R. Stenberg, a Texan who was less charitable than Abernethy in his analysis of Jackson's motives. In a series of articles published in the 1930's, Stenberg drew a harsh portrayal of Jackson as a treacherous politician who was hypocritical and self-seeking

---

ward Channing," *Massachusetts Historical Society Proceedings*, LXIV, 250-84; J. A. DeNovo, "Edward Channing's 'Great Work' Twenty Years After," *Mississippi Valley Historical Review*, XXXIX, 257-74; Kraus, 232-41; Wish, 127-30.

and who at the same time "was vindictive and narrow in his personal relationships.[19]

Turner's interpretation of the Jacksonian movement was also mildly criticized by several pro-Jacksonian scholars who felt that his interpretation underplayed the importance of class struggle and urban labor radicalism in Jacksonian politics by placing too much emphasis upon the West and the sectional conflict. These scholars called for an appreciation of the role played by the Eastern labor movement in shaping the Jacksonian appeal.

Though the work of Ely and of McMaster helped pave the way for the new "urban labor thesis," the publication of *Social Forces in American History* by the socialist publicist, Algie M. Simons, provided the first comprehensive statement of the hypothesis that Eastern labor, rather than the Western frontier, constituted the truly creative egalitarian wing of Jacksonian Democracy. Simons' Marxist orientation led him to place special emphasis upon the trade union movement of the Jacksonian era. He found that movement "measured by the impress it left . . . the most important event in American history." Unlike some later scholars, however, Simons did not find the labor movement in control of the Jacksonian party. The Jackson movement, he contended, was actually an incompatible coalition composed of both "the rising bourgeoisie" and "the class conscious proletariat." The Jacksonians, in

19. Abernethy, "Andrew Jackson and the Rise of Southwestern Democracy," *American Historical Review*, XXXIII, 64-77; "The Origin of the Whig Party in Tennessee," *Mississippi Valley Historical Review*, XII, 504-22; *From Frontier to Plantation in Tennessee: A Study in Frontier Democracy* (Chapel Hill, 1932), pp. 238-49. Stenberg, "Jackson, Anthony Butler, and Texas," *Southwestern Social Science Quarterly*, XIII, 264-86; "Jackson, Buchanan and the 'Corrupt Bargain' Calumny," *Pennsylvania Magazine of History and Biography*, LVIII, 61-85; "The Texas Schemes of Jackson and Houston, 1829-1836," *Southwestern Social Science Quarterly*, XV, 229-50; "Jackson's 'Rhea Letter' Hoax," *Journal of Southern History*, II, 480-96; "Jackson's Neches Claims, 1829-1836," *Southwestern Historical Quarterly* XXXIX, 255-74; "Andrew Jackson and the Erving Affidavit," *Ibid.*, XLI, 142-53; "President Jackson and Anthony Butler," *Southwest Review*, XXII, 391-404; "A Note on the Jackson-Calhoun Breach of 1830-1831," *Tyler's Quarterly Historical and Genelogical Magazine*, XXI, 65-69. According to Charles G. Sellers, Stenberg planned to publish an exposé of Old Hickory to be entitled, *The Insidious Andrew Jackson*. The book never appeared. Charles G. Sellers, "Andrew Jackson versus the Historians," *Mississippi Valley Historical Review*, XLIV, 615-34. For a critique of Abernethy's analysis of Jackson's role in Tennessee politics see Sellers, "Banking and Politics in Jackson's Tennessee," *Ibid.*, XLI, 61-84. For Turner's answer to Channing, see his posthumous *The United States, 1830-1850* (New York, 1935), pp. 31-36.

his judgment, were generally bourgeois in their essential attitudes. However, he argued, the proletarian labor elements constituted an important, historically significant minority protest movement within Democratic ranks. Idealizing those proletarian elements, Simons deprecated Turner's praise of frontier democracy. "The frontier," he wrote, "which is spoken of as being ascendant under Jackson was distinctly individualistic and small capitalist in its instincts, rather than proletarian." The truly significant contribution to American development in Jackson's day, Simons declared, came not from the frontier, but from the cities, where the wage workers, "fired into brief activity," first came to possess "that sense of coming social power which alone gave the class consciousness necessary to effective opportunity." He found the Jacksonian movement as a whole, however, rather devoid of that class consciousness. "It was neither frontier, nor wage working, nor even purely capitalist in its makeup," he concluded. "It can better be described as the 'democracy' of expectant capitalists.' It borrowed something from the frontier. The brutality, coarseness, admiration for boorishness and ignorance, have been especially ascribed to the frontier, but they belong equally well to crude, competitive capitalism."[20]

Though non-Marxist liberal historians generally rejected Simons' view of the conflict between the minority proletarian groups and the dominant, bourgeois, "expectant capitalist" elements within the Jackson camp, numerous specialized studies published during the first four decades of the twentieth century gave impetus to the demand for a revision of Turner's conception of the frontier origins of Jacksonian Democracy. Arthur C. Cole's classic monograph *The Whig Party in the South* found party divisions in the southern United States prior to the Civil War essentially a reflection of class divisions. The southern Whigs, in his analysis, were primarily a party of wealth, respectability, and conservatism, while the southern Democrats represented the poor white, the yeoman, the small planter, and the small slaveholder. The history of the American

20. *Social Forces in American History* (New York, 1911), pp. 179-90, 209-10. An earlier, less complete statement of Simons' interpretation of the Jackson era may be found in his *Class Struggles in America* (Chicago, 1906). On Simons social philosophy, see Eric Goldman, *Rendevous with Destiny* (New York, 1953), pp. 141-43; William A. Glaser, "Algie Martin Simons and Marxism in America," *Missippi Valley Historical Review*, XLI, 419-34. In his later writings, Frederick Jackson Turner also spoke of the Jacksonian West as a competitive, "expectant capitalist" society. *The United States, 1830-1850*, p. 20.

labor movement published by John R. Commons and his associates emphasized the importance of the urban workingmen's party in sustaining the more radical, antimonopoly wing of the Jacksonian party. "During the entire trade union period," wrote Edward Middleman, (the author of that portion of the Commons study which dealt with the Jacksonian labor movement), "the workingmen, together with the master mechanics and small tradesmen who also felt the sting of corporations and banks, had agitated against these so-called monopolies. The fight which Jackson had led on the United States Bank was the latest glorious example." Middleman found that the political activism of the Eastern urban groups, not the influence of the frontier, contributed the most to strengthening the more idealistic, reform-minded elements within the Jacksonian coalition.[21]

The studies of the New York Locofoco movement published by William Trimble, a graduate student in Turner's Harvard seminar, supported Middleman's conclusions. Though Trimble adhered to the teachings of Turner in finding the "Democratic party of the time . . . essentially agrarian," he regarded the class antagonisms of urban and industrial America as the source of the Locofoco's dissidence and labelled their organization "in reality a nascent proletarian movement." He also found this fringe group closer to true Jeffersonian idealism and more genuinely egalitarian than the main body of the Democratic party. Trimble suggested that it was only when Locofoco precepts gained the ascendency within the national organization during the Van Buren administration that "the Democratic Republican party . . . began to become (at least in the North) the modern Democratic party." "Modern industrialism and the Democratic party," he concluded, "developed contemporaneously." In Trimble's view, the urban radicalism of the Locofoco, not the egalitarianism of the frontier, provided the greatest support to Democratic idealism during the Jacksonian years.[22]

21. *The Whig Party in the South* (Washington, 1913), pp. 53, 58, 69, 70, 71, 72, 104; Commons (ed.), *The History of Labour in the United States* (2 vols., New York, 1918), I, 458-59. Much the same interpretation may be found in Nathan Fine, *Labor and Farmer Parties in the United States, 1828-1928* (New York, 1928); in Alden Whitman, *Labor Parties, 1827-1834* (New York, 1943); and in Louis M. Hacker, *The Triumph of American Capitalism* (New York, 1940).

22. "Diverging Tendencies in New York Democracy in the Period of the Locofocos," *American Historical Review*, XXIV, 396-421; "The Social Philosophy of the Locofoco Democracy," *The American Journal of Sociology*, XXVI, 705-15.

Columbia professor Dixon Ryan Fox, in his *Decline of Aristocracy in the Politics of New York*, concluded that political affiliations in the Empire State during the Jacksonian years were determined primarily by economic status, got geography. Analyzing voting in the larger cities of the state, Fox found that "where property valuation *per capita* was relatively large, the ward was Whig . . . where mechanics made their home, democratic candidates generally were certain of election." Henry R. Mueller's study of *The Whig Party in Pennsylvania* found the Whig cause solidly supported by the prosperous. "The conclusion is almost inevitable," he wrote, "that although the Whigs did not include all the wealth of the state, yet the vast majority of those possessing vested interests felt that the Whig party offered them more protection than did the opposition party." E. Malcolm Carroll's *Origins of the Whig Party* concurred in finding the Whig organization the vehicle of propertied classes instinctively hostile to the aspirations of the rising labor movement. Reginald McGrane, in his monograph *The Panic of 1837*, followed Trimble in perceiving in the Locofoco movement an expression of the conflict "between capital and labor." Henry H. Simms, a student of Fox at Columbia, declared in his *Rise of the Whigs in Virginia, 1824-1840* that "the struggle between the Jackson and anti-Jacksonian forces was in large part a class struggle. Jackson, unlike Jefferson, was a social democrat. . . . The principle opposition to Jackson in the state came from conservative classes, from men possessed of property in slaves or otherwise, who refused to accept either his brand of nationalism or his theory of democracy." Simms, finding no evidence that Jacksonian political strength was centered in frontier areas, concluded that the real theme of the Jacksonian period was "the struggle between the leveling tendencies of Jacksonian democracy and the conservative elements possessed of property." Philip S. Klein's *Pennsylvania Politics, 1817-1832: A Game without Rules* found the opposition to Jackson in Pennsylvania led and supported by the more affluent and respectable citizens of that commonwealth.[23]

Not all specialized studies of Jacksonian politics, however, sup-

23. *The Decline of Aristocracy in the Politics of New York* (New York, 1919), pp. 422, 426, 429, 431, 436-38; *The Whig Party in Pennsylvania* (New York, 1922), pp. 243-45; *The Origins of the Whig Party* (Durham, 1925), pp. 170-227; *The Panic of 1837* (Chicago, 1924), p. 149; *The Rise of the Whigs in Virginia, 1824-1840* (Richmond, 1929), pp. 36, 165-66; *Pennsylvania Politics, 1817-1832: A Game Without Rules* (Harrisburg, 1940), pp. 226-27.

ported the conclusions reached by Commons, Fox, Simms, Trimble, and other critics of the "frontier democracy" thesis. Arthur B. Darling's investigations of the origins and nature of the so-called "Workingmen's party" of Massachusetts suggested than, in the Bay State at any rate, the Turner hypothesis offered the most feasible explanation of Jacksonian Democracy. Darling charged that earlier interpreters, notably the authors of the Commons' study, had made serious errors in their analysis of the Jacksonian "labor" movement. The Workingmen's party, he found, was "not representative of an urban and industrial proletariat in Massachusetts." Rather, it was "preponderantly a rural and agrarian party, with an urban complement of carpenters, masons and ship caulkers, the mechanics of those days." To support his contention that the movement was primarily rural, not urban, Darling pointed to the fact that the workingmen's party consistently polled a higher percentage of the vote in the Western areas of the state than in the urban Boston. As for the Jacksonian party itself, Darling argued that although it did command stronger support from the lower classes than from the propertied, the "largest group in the Democratic party was the small farming class of the Western and Southern counties." He concluded that the Jacksonian movement was, as Turner suggested, essentially an agrarian movement commanding only incidental urban labor support.[24]

Darling's dissent notwithstanding, several eminent scholars during the 1920's demanded a general reinterpretation of the Jacksonian movement which would do justice to the decisive role presumably played by urban labor in the politics of the Jacksonian era. In 1922, Arthur M. Schlesinger, at that time a professor of history at the University of Iowa, argued, in an essay entitled "The Significance of Jacksonian Democracy," that both "the rise of a new society in the West" and the "development of a dynamic labor movement in the East" were of major importance in the Jacksonian crusade. "Indeed," Schlesinger wrote, "[Jackson] could not have been elected president if the votes of the laboring men of the Northeast had not been added to those of his followers in the Southeast and the West. Jackson capitalized on this support when

24. "Jacksonian Democracy in Massachusetts, 1821-1848," *American Historical Review*, XIX, 271-87, "The Workingman's Party in Massachusetts, 1833-1834," *Ibid.*, XXIX, 81-86; *Political Changes in Massachusetts, 1824-1848* (New Haven, 1925).

he waged battle against the great financial monopoly, the Bank of the United States, and gave express recognition to its demands when he established the ten-hour workday in the federal shipyards in 1836." The labor movement, reflecting the increasing urban distress which followed in the wake of the incipient industrialization of the 1830's, in Schlesinger's analysis provided the winning ingredient in the Jacksonian political coalition.[25]

Charles A. Beard, the controversial author of *An Economic Interpretation of the Constitution of the United States,* joined Schlesinger in calling for a new interpretation of the Jacksonian era which would emphasize the struggle of economic classes as well as the sectional conflict in Jacksonian politics. In a book review published in *The New Republic* in 1921, Beard had expressed serious misgivings concerning the frontier thesis. Turner's approach to the American past, he protested, tended to blur more vital class antagonisms while overemphasizing less important sectional and geographical factors. The real dynamic force underlying American party battles, Beard suggested, would be found in the conflict, not of sections, but of economic interests. In the late 1920's, in collaboration with his wife, Mary, he sought to correct this presumed distortion as it applied to the Jacksonian era by proclaiming, in *The Rise of American Civilization,* that the Jacksonian movement was in fact "a triumphant farmer-labor party" which constituted the "radical left wing" of Jeffersonian Republicanism. Like Schlesinger, the Beards did not totally discard Turner's emphasis upon the crucial role played by sectionalism in American politics, but argued that the Jacksonians added to the old Jeffersonian alliance of Western farmers and Southern agrarians the laboring classes of the large Eastern cities. Those laboring classes, in Beard's view, were in the Jackson era just beginning to develop a militant class consciousness. In *The Economic Basis of Politics,* first published in 1928, Beard argued that by opposing the neo-Hamiltonian, property-oriented policies espoused by Clay and Adams, particularly in their support of Bank recharter, "Jackson made himself the open champion of the humbler members of society, the farmers, mechanics, and laborers, against the rich and powerful."[26]

25. *New Viewpoints in American History* (New York, 1922), pp. 201-18.
26. "The Frontier in American History," *The New Republic,* XXV, 349-50; *The Rise of American Civilization* (New York, 1927), I, 557; *The Economic Basis of Politics and Related Writings* (New York, 1957), pp. 184-93. A very

Beard's writings were infused with a strong and outspoken Jacksonian partisanship. In his interpretation, the party battles of the Jackson period were a dualistic struggle between the Jacksonian determination to protect the "humbler members of society" from exploitation and the Whig conspiracy to further the interests of the "rich and powerful . . . the financial and industrial interests of New England and the Middle States." He dismissed Whig claims of fidelity to Jeffersonian and democratic principles as sheer cant: "There was no doubt about the measures which the Whig leaders supported in their hearts. In their program, the Federalist creed was repeated in full, or rather, continued unbroken." Regarding the opponents of Jackson as the servants of the vested economic interests of the conservative, propertied classes, Beard strongly intimated that their program was inherently hostile to the economic interests of the great majority of Americans. In his treatment of the Jackson era, the transition from the anti-Jacksonian partisanship of Gilded Age historiography to the new celebration of the Jacksonians as virtuous champions of the common man was made complete.[27]

A less enthusiastically partisan analysis of Jacksonian Democracy was provided by the great scholar of American literature Vernon Louis Parrington. Parrington, a former Populist, was closer to Turner's agrarian idealism than Beard. However, he fully shared Beard's conviction that class antagonisms lay at the root of the Jacksonian movement. Jackson's "motley following of Western agrarians and Eastern proletarians," Parrington declared, were determined to arrest the flow of "the waters of prosperity . . . into private hands through governmental pipelines." "The assault on the Bank" expressed their resentment over the fact that "in practice the mains seemed to conduct only to Lowell industrialists and Philadelphia and New York capitalists." "The driving force of

perceptive analysis of the specific ethic groups and social classes which supported the Jacksonian coalition was provided several years later in Wilfred E. Binkley, *American Political Parties, Their Natural History* (New York, 1943), pp. 120-41. Binkley's conclusions supported a modified class interpretation of the Jacksonian movement.

27. Beard, *Economic Basis of Politics*, pp. 188-92. Excellent critiques of Beard as an historian are provided in Maurice Blenkoff, *The Influence of Charles A. Beard Upon American Historiography* (Buffalo, 1936); Howard K. Beale (ed.), *Charles A. Beard* (University of Kentucky, 1954); Cushing Stout, *The Pragmatic Revolt in American Historiography* (New Haven, 1958); and Lee Benson, *Turner and Beard* (Glencoe, Ill., 1960). See also Wish, pp. 265-92 and Kraus, pp. 367-74.

the new democracy," Parrington declared, "was the same class feeling that had done service a generation before, the will to destroy the aristocratic principle in government."[28]

Parrington's emotional sympathies were most decidedly on the side of Jackson and his followers. Old Hickory, he declared with feeling, "was one of our few Presidents whose heart and sympathies were with the plain people, and who clung to the simple faith that the government must deal as justly with the poor as with the rich." However, he expressed two serious reservations concerning Jacksonian Democracy. He found the movement devoid of any political philosophy adequate to cope with the changing circumstances of the new era "As [his] policy unfolded, it became clear that Jackson had not changed with changing times. He remained to the last the product of an earlier domestic economy, with an old fashioned horror of debt . . . in his attitude toward the Bank, as in his attitude toward internal improvements, Jackson returned to the agrarian position of Jefferson and John Taylor, nullifying for a time the victories gained by the middle class during the boom period of nationalism. The more he learned about the methods of capitalistic finance, the more he distrusted it." Under Jacksonian aegis, Parrington contended, "the American people were wanting in an adequate democratic program suited to the changing times." Parrington also found that, because of internal contradictions within the Jacksonian camp, the democratic impulse of the Jacksonian era ultimately proved inadequate for the preservation of the simple agrarian egalitarian republic of Jefferson. He lamented the betrayal of the Jeffersonian-Jacksonian ideal by politicians who "used the movement for narrow partisan ends" and added, rather bitterly, "Perhaps the rarest bit of irony in American history is the later custodianship of democracy by the middle class, who, while perfecting their tariffs and subsidies, legislating from the bench, exploiting the state and outlawing all political theories but their own, denounce all class consciousness as unpatriotic and all agrarian programs as undemocratic." Parrington did not, however, allow his belief that Jacksonian Democracy had failed to alter his high regard for the simple agrarian idealism of Old Hickory. "It was no fault of Andrew Jackson if the final outcome of the great movement of Jacksonian Democracy was so untoward; it was

28. *Main Currents in American Thought* (New York, 1954), II, 138-44. (This was first published in 1926).

49

rather the fault of the times that they were not ripe for democracy."[29]

In Parrington's work, as in Turner's, there are strong undercurrents of nostalgia for the Jeffersonian past, for the idealism and simplicity of the earlier republic. Parrington's interpretation of the Age of Jackson argued in effect that Jacksonian America, in its eagerness to build a capitalist paradise by unleasing middle-class individualism, destroyed the Jeffersonian heritage.

If Beard and Parrington retained much of the Turner conception of Jacksonian Democracy in their work, Arthur Schlesinger, Jr., whose Pulitzer prize winning *Age of Jackson* appeared in 1945, rejected most of Turner's theorizings. "More can be understood about Jacksonian Democracy," Schlesinger wrote, "if it is regarded as a problem not of sections but of classes." Taking issue with the frontier hypothesis, he followed earlier advocates of the urban labor interpretation of Jacksonian Democracy in regarding the cities of the East, rather than the pioneer settlements of the West, as the birthplace of the most creative and progressive Jacksonian conceptions. Schlesinger found the labor groups of the Eastern urban centers, of all the groups within the Jacksonian coalition, the most determined in their efforts to attain social justice through restraining corporate power, enacting maximum hours legislation and labor lien laws, fostering public education, and abolishing imprisonment for debt. In a striking reversal of Turner's praise for the classless society of the West as the cradle of democratic idealism, Schlesinger argued that the very lack of hard and fast class distinctions rendered the Western Jacksonians indifferent to the real need for economic reform. "The new quest for economic democracy meant little to men of the West, however deeply they cared about political and civil freedoms . . . living amidst conditions of substantial equality with limitless vistas of economic opportunity before them, [they] aimed more at establishing local self-government and majority rule than at safeguarding the material foundations of political democracy." The Eastern laborers, on the other hand, threatened with the destruction of their status and plagued by

29. *Ibid.*, II, 142-43. For critical analyses of Parrington's work, see William T. Utler, "Vernon Louis Parrington," *Jernegan Essays*, pp. 394-408; Richard Hofstadter, "Parrington and the Jeffersonian Tradition," *Journal of the History of Ideas*, II, 391-400; Arthur A. Ekirch, Jr., "Parrington and the Decline of American Liberalism," *American Quarterly*, III, 295-308; Kraus, 350-55; Wish, 295-307.

nagging insecurity, were of necessity more "sensitive to economic issues." Out of their sensitivity to the need for reform came the true contribution of the Jacksonian movement to the American liberal heritage.[30]

Schlesinger thus found the essential meaning of the Jacksonian upheaval in its economic, rather than in its political, objectives. The motivating force behind Jacksonian policies, Schlesinger argued, was the determination of "farmers and laborers" to use their newly won political power to gain freedom from economic exploitation in a society increasingly dominated by business interests. Their resolution to "control the capitalist groups," in Schlesinger's analysis, constituted the key to comprehending the Jacksonian era. Regarding the Jacksonians as the nineteenth-century precursors of twentieth-century liberal reform movements, he lauded their realization that the non-capitalist groups in American society must unite to use their power, not to destroy capitalism, but "to keep the capitalists from destroying it." Though Schlesinger found that the Jacksonians came to this realization slowly and never really formulated a philosophical justification of their course of action, he argued that their struggles against the Bank of the United States and the American System, as well as their demands for state control and regulation of banking and business, represented a pragmatic acceptance of the necessity to restrain, through governmental action, the selfish proclivities of the business class. It was Schlesinger's contention that the Jacksonians, though believing in the Jeffersonian creed of limited government, were driven by the necessity of events to espouse, in increasing measure, the adoption of Hamiltonian means to attain Jeffersonian ends. Though they never fully appreciated the implications of this development, "the Jacksonians under the banner of antistatism [carried] on a vigorous program of government intervention" designed to check the growing power of the business community. It was therefore no accident that "Jackson, ruling in the name of weak government, ended up by leaving the Presidency stronger than it had ever been before." In Schlesinger's analysis, this development was inevitable, for the Jacksonians were caught up in "the irrepressible conflict of capitalism: the struggle on the part of the business community to dominate the state, and on the part of the rest of society, under

30. *The Age of Jackson* (Boston, 1945), pp. 57-59, 142, 189, 205-9, 257, 262-63, 301, 505, 514.

the leadership of 'liberals,' to check the political ambitions of business."[31]

In essence, Schlesinger's interpretation of the Jacksonian movement argued that, despite their bondage to the "antistatist" assumptions of the Jeffersonians, the Jacksonian Democrats, by throwing the weight of the federal government into the balance to check the power of corporate wealth (as symbolized by Nicholas Biddle's Second Bank of the United States) in effect began the "redirection" of American liberalism. With the coming of Jackson, American liberals, Schlesinger submitted, came to accept concepts of positive government in practice if not in profession. In that sense, the Jacksonians contributed mightily to that historic struggle "on the part of the other segments of society to restrain the power of the business community," which, in Schlesinger's view, constituted one of the major themes of American history. Schlesinger candidly admitted his deep, partisan commitment to that struggle. If Bancroft's volumes on Colonial and Revolutionary America voted for Jackson, Arthur Schlesinger, Jr.'s *Age of Jackson* voted for Franklin Delano Roosevelt.[32]

Jacksonian historiography during the first four and a half decades of the twentieth century was thus largely dominated by historians sympathetic to the Jacksonian movement, although they differed

31. *Ibid.*, pp. 509-23. In interpreting Jacksonian Democracy as an essentially "anti-capitalist" movement grounded in class antagonisms and directed to the restraint, though not the destruction, of the capitalist classes, Schlesinger by no means ignored the fact that there were many within the Jacksonian fold who accepted no such program. Indeed, perhaps no historian has been more aware than Schlesinger of the essential pluralism and diversity of the party of Jackson and Van Buren. But in Schlesinger's judgment the state banking interests who opposed the hard-money policy, the Western Jacksonians who supported the American System and the Southern planters who harbored hostility to egalitarian democracy, though numerous, were not in the main stream of the Jacksonian movement. The true spokesmen of the Jacksonian faith, to Schlesinger, were not the Nathan P. Tallmadges and the David Henshaws, devoted to personal profit and motivated by sheer opportunism, nor the Calhouns pledged to the defense of slavery. They were rather the Van Burens, the Wrights, and the Bancrofts dedicated to the true interests of the common people of the land. Schlesinger found Jacksonian idealism dominant, Jacksonian conservatism and opportunism secondary in the great democratic crusade. As we shall see in the next chapter, very few contemporary historians share Schlesinger's fervid belief in Jacksonian idealism. Pp. 43, 59, 115, 119, 122, 169, 239.

32. It should, perhaps, be mentioned that though Schlesinger's interpretation of the party battles of the Jackson era made use of an economic theory of politics, his total analysis was by no means grounded in a narrow economic

as to the nature and origins of Jacksonian Democracy. Frank Freidel has pointed out that, though text-book writers frequently followed the earlier, anti-Jackson interpretation, the majority of scholars working in the Jackson era portrayed Old Hickory as the guardian of the Democratic faith. This spirit of Jacksonian partisanship was most pronounced, not only in the widely read scholarly works of Charles A. Beard and Arthur M. Schlesinger, Jr., but also in two best-selling popular surveys of the Jackson era, Claude Bowers' *Party Battles of the Jackson Period*, published in 1922 and Marquis James' *Andrew Jackson: Portrait of A President*, which appeared in 1937. These vivid accounts brought the revisionist, pro-Jacksonian interpretations of Old Hickory and the Jacksonian movement to millions of readers.[33]

---

determinism. A pragmatist and a pluralist in his approach to history, Schlesinger dismissed the notion that historical causation can be explained solely in terms of class antagonisms. He placed much emphasis on intellectual and moral considerations as causative factors in history, and rather firmly rejected the Marxist and Beardian interpretations of the causes of the Civil War. Though stressing the presence of deep class consciousness in the Jackson era, he refused to allow this concern with class antagonisms to harden into a narrowly monistic interpretation of history. Pp. 86, 432.

33. Freidel, 41-52; *Party Battles of the Jackson Period* (New York, 1922); *Andrew Jackson, Portrait of a President* (New York, 1937). See also H. R. Fraser, *Democracy in the Making* (Indianapolis, 1938).

3. RECENT TRENDS IN JACKSONIAN HISTORIOGRAPHY

D uring the past decade and a half, few aspects of the American past have provoked as much scholarly controversy, or been subjected to as much searching reappraisal, as the Jacksonian era. There has been little consensus among historians concerning the nature of the Jacksonian movement and its influence in the main stream of American life. There has, however, been a pronounced tendency to question the validity of the pro-Democratic, pro-Jacksonian interpretations advanced by the historians of the previous generation.

The publication in 1945 of Arthur Schlesinger, Jr.'s *Age of Jackson* acted as a catalyst to the new revisionism. Perhaps the most controversial aspect of Schlesinger's volume was its emphasis upon the importance of a militantly class-conscious Eastern labor movement in shaping the more radical aspects of the Jacksonian program. Almost immediately, other scholars came forward to take issue with Schlesinger's interpretation of the nature and importance of the Jacksonian labor movement. Professor Joseph Dorfman of Columbia University argued that the so-called "workingmen's movement" of the Jackson era did not actually represent urban labor at all. The "labor" spokesmen of the 1830's, Dorfman contended, were in reality nascent entrepreneurs who enunciated, not the demands of a submerged proletariat, but the program of the businessman on the make. Pointing to their advocacy of strict laissez faire and of limited governmental activity, he argued that these so-called "radicals" offered little to the "permanent wage earning class" but rather served the cause of those business groups who desired freedom from mercantilistic restrictions and special privilege. He found these 'labor spokesmen' almost totally indifferent to questions concerning the hours, wages, and conditions of labor. The objective of the Jacksonian party "was not to help labor—they generally neglected labor reform—but to create better business conditions."[1]

1. "The Jackson Wage-Earner Thesis," *American Historical Review*, LIV, 296-306. The "Wage-Earner" article, originally delivered as a paper at the

Dorfman charged that Schlesinger and earlier historians of the Jackson labor movement had been led astray by their failure to appreciate the fact that, during the Jacksonian era, the term "workingman" was not used to denote only wage earners or members of a proletariat, but was rather applied indiscriminately to anyone who engaged in any form of useful activity. "Only your political opponents and the terrible aristocrats and the lazy idlers were clearly not 'honest workingmen.' "[2]

The key to understanding the Jackson era, Dorfman argued, lay not in regarding the party battles of the day as expressions of antagonisms between social classes, but rather as seeing them as internecine feuds fought within the business community. "The so-called labor movement . . . .was antiaristocratic rather than anticapitalistic. . . . The humanitarian element contributed a weak impress of reform, but it was decidedly thrown into the shade by the business drive." The very political measures which Schlesinger interpreted as evidence of a Jacksonian determination to restrain the business community Dorfman saw as an expression of that "business drive." "The movement is a liberal one in the sense that it sought to eliminate or hedge law-created privileges. And it was anticapitalist only in the sense that it opposed the special advantages and sudden wealth that a few capitalists, or even down-at-the-heel adventurers or blue bloods, could secure by favoritism, the manipulation of political power, intrigue, or ingratiation with the powers that be. After all, the Age of Jackson was an age of expansion, a great age of business enterprise, and the body of capitalists, enterprisers, and ambitious workingmen were not prepared to abandon the race to the type of political capitalists just described." Dorfman concluded that Schlesinger and other pro-Jacksonian scholars had sought to mould the Jacksonian movement into the pattern of later liberal reform movements and in so doing had missed the true meaning of the Jacksonian antimonopoly crusade. "It will not do," Dorfman enjoined, "to read into the history of American radicalism, at least for the Jackson period, the later con-

---

American Historical Association 1946 convention, was published in the *Review* three years later. The above citations are from the version in the *Review*. Dorfman's interpretation of Jacksonian Democracy may also be found, in less explicit form, in *The Economic Mind in American Civilization* (New York, 1946), II, 637-95.

2. "The Jackson Wage-Earner Thesis," pp. 296-306.

ception of a class conflict between the great capitalists on the one side, and a mass of propertyless wage earners on the other." The Jacksonians, in his judgment, represented middle-class entrepreneurial aspirations, not lower-class proletarian grievances.[3]

Other studies of the Jacksonian relationship to labor lent support to Dorfman's conclusions. Richard B. Morris, also of Columbia University, in an article entitled "Andrew Jackson, Strikebreaker," pointed out that Jackson was the first President to call for federal troops to quell a labor disturbance. He concluded that "there is no evidence that Jackson favored combinations of labor any more than combinations of capital or that he approved of the strike weapon." Morris' revelation that Jackson's close political associate, John H. Eaton, held the presidency of the corporation involved in the dispute lent some credence to the entrepreneurial interpretation of the Jackson movement.[4]

Further support for that interpretation was offered by William A. Sullivan, a graduate student of Morris at Columbia. Sullivan, analyzing voting behavior in Philadelphia during the Jacksonian years, found no evidence that the working class tended to vote for Jackson or for candidates of the Jacksonian party. Comparing property valuations and voting returns by wards, he concluded: "The workingmen of Philadelphia gave their votes far more consistently to the Whigs than to the Jacksonian Democrats. Moreover, it was prior to the Bank War and not during it that the working class revealed any inclination to follow the lead of Jackson and his party."[5]

Edward Pessen, also a student of Morris, undertook a similar analysis of voting behavior in Boston. He found that "Andrew Jackson himself was not supported at the polls by the workingmen . . . It was not until the mid-thirties, at the end of his second term, that his party was able to win small majorities in any of the working class wards." Pessen also investigated the so-called "Workingmen's party" of Massachusetts. He found its membership motivated, not by militantly proletarian class consciousness, but by "middle class

3. *Ibid.*, p. 306.
4. "Andrew Jackson, Strikebreaker," *American Historical Review*, LV, 54-68. See also Morris' article, " 'Old Hickory Jackson' was no FDR," *Labor and Nation*, V, 38-40.
5. "Did Labor Support Andrew Jackson?" *Political Science Quarterly*, XLII, 569-80. See also Sullivan's *The Industrial Worker in Pennsylvania, 1800-1840* (Harrisburg, 1955).

aspirations." After discovering that many of the wealthiest men in the community, Whigs in known political affiliation, received the Workingmen's Party endorsement, Pessen conjectured that this party may have been, "a front organization for the Whigs."[6]

In a later article on "The Workingmen's Movement of the Jacksonian Era," however, Pessen concluded that the Workingmen's parties in the Eastern urban centers generally expressed a very genuine demand for social reforms designed to better the condition of the laborer. Though the parties were not composed exclusively of laborers and included many diverse elements (among them not a few opportunists) he suggested that their "very existence" nonetheless "exasperated that section of the business community which liked to think that merchants and capitalists, too, were workingmen." After a careful analysis of the social ideas of labor spokesmen, Pessen found in the ranks of the Workingmen's organizations radical spokesmen who preached the doctrine of class conflict, denounced the domination of society by the wealthy, and called for a sweeping transformation in social organization. However, he concluded that the labor parties as a whole were reformist, not revolutionary, and far from representing a militant proletariat they were rather affected by "the mood of the American workingmen of that era: a man who while a worker today might become a master tomorrow; a man who dreamed of ascending into a higher social station as he simultaneously demanded the right to organize and strike." In sharp contrast with the interpretation advanced by Arthur Schlesinger, Jr., Pessen submitted, after a careful study of the pronouncements of Workingmen's party spokesmen concerning the partisan battles of the Jackson era, that these groups, far from being militantly pro-Jacksonian, "often displayed indifference if not actual hostility" toward the Democratic party. In explanation of this lack of staunch labor support, Pessen argued that the Jacksonian party as a whole was not actually firmly dedicated to the reformism espoused by the emergent labor groups. "If the Jacksonian movement," he declared, "was in fact a movement primarily devoted to achieving a freer competitive capitalism, workingmen certainly had demands which went far beyond that objective." Pessen therefore rejected Schlesinger's equation of the Jacksonian party and the reform impulse of the Age of Jackson.[7]

6. "Did Labor Support Andrew Jackson? The Boston Story," *Political Science Quarterly*, LXIV, 262-74.

The revisionist interpretation of the Jacksonian labor movement was given further expression in Walter Hugins' monographic study of the New York Workingmen's movement. Taking issue with the Trimble interpretation of the Locofocos, Hugins followed Dorfman in arguing that the so-called labor groups were neither motivated by a proletarian sense of class injustice nor expressive of anti-capitalist setiment. Rather, in Hugins' judgment, the movement reflected the determination of newly enfranchised commoners of all classes—"journeymen and masters, manufacturers and merchants"—to obtain a share of the largess of capitalist society by destroying the last vestiges of special privilege which barred the way to economic advancement. Hugins found that the Workingmen's movement in New York, for example, far from representing a nascent proletariat, drew support from a broad stratum of society ranging from the wage earners to the professions. In his view, it sought not to challenge the emerging business economy, but rather to assist "mechanics and small businessmen to further the democratization of this capitalist society, making more of its fruits available to all." Its adherents, then, were moved, not by "proletarian animosity to the existing order, but [by] the desire for equal opportunity to become capitalists themselves." The movement, in Hugins' interpretation, gave expression to the capitalistic instincts of merchants and manufacturers stifled by the mercantilistic restrictions of the old order as well as to the status aspirations of the less privileged.[8]

In arriving at these rather controversial conclusions, Hugins employed a three-fold approach. First, he carefully analyzed the existing biographical data concerning some seven hundred individuals active in the movement. He found that their spokesmen were

7. "The Workingmen's Movement of the Jacksonian Era." *Mississippi Valley Historical Review*, XLIII, 428-43. See also Edward Pessen, "The Social Philosophy of Early American Leaders of Labor" (Ph.D. dissertation, Columbia University, 1954); "Thomas Skidmore, Agrarian Reformer in the Early American Labor Movement," *New York History*, XXV, 280-96; "The Ideology of Stephen Simpson, Upper Class Champion of the Early Philadelphia Workingmen's Movement," *Pennsylvania History*, XXII, 328-40. For a recent restatement of the Marxist interpretation of the Jacksonian labor movement as an incipient expression of proletarian class consciousness, see Philip S. Foner, *History of the Labor Movement in the United States* (New York, 1947), pp. 121-66.

8. Hugins, *Jacksonian Democracy and the Working Class: A Study of the New York Workingmen's Movement* (Stanford, 1960), pp. 8, 80, 112-28, 132-202, 208-20, 223, 263.

drawn, not from the laboring class alone, but from all walks of life. They represented, he wrote, a "microcosmic cross section of New York society." (He did, however, find evidence to indicate that there was little participation in the movement at the upper and lower extremes of the economic scale, evidence which reinforced his interpretation of the movement as essentially middle class in aspiration.) Then, in analyzing their program, Hugins confirmed Dorfman's contention that their demands were geared, not to the needs of labor, but to the aspirations of that portion of the business community injured by "aristocratic" restrictions on enterprise. Finally, in analyzing election returns, Hugins discovered that though the wards of lower property valuation tended to supply a higher proportion of the Workingmen and Locofoco votes than did the more prosperous wards, their supporters were nonetheless distributed throughout the city. That, he concluded, belied the assertion "that this was a class movement in any sense."[9]

The thesis that the workingmen's movement of the Jacksonian era reflected capitalist aspirations rather than class antagonisms has not, however, won the complete acceptance of Jacksonian scholars. Pessen's reservations concerning this "entrepreneurial" interpretation of the Jacksonian labor groups have already been noted. Another student of the period, Louis Arky of the University of Pennsylvania, in an article dealing with "The Mechanics' Union of Trade Associations and the Formation of the Philadelphia Workingmen's Movement," found the spokesmen of labor in that city in 1828-29 "possessed of a monomania against capitalists." Tracing their ideology to the Richardian socialists' labor theory of value, Arky found in the workingmen's movement an expression of alienation from the emergent business order, not enthusiastic acceptance of middle class values. Outlining the objectives of the movement, Arky wrote: "They sought to arrest the momentum of incipient capitalism, using a tool they were not adept in wielding: the apparatus of government. The workingmen wished to revert to an economy of small production wherein the worker was identified with his product in the community. They desired to assert their individualism at a time when new methods of production would force them into a stereotype."[10]

9. *Ibid.* See also Hugins' article. "Ely Moore: The Case History of a Jacksonian Labor Leader," *Political Science Quarterly,* LXV, 105-25.
10. "The Mechanics' Union of Trade Associations and the Formation of the

Other scholars challenged the statistical methodology of the labor studies. Arthur Schlesinger, Jr., replying to Joseph Dorfman's criticisms of his interpretation of the Jacksonian movement, questioned the assumption that proof of the presence of businessmen within the Jacksonian camp effectively refuted the contention that the primary reform objective of the 1830's was the restraint of the capitalist class. "Of course," Schlestinger wrote, "many businessmen were pro-Jackson, as many businessmen were pro-Roosevelt; of course, many supporters of the working class in Jackson's day were not themselves workingmen, any more than they are today; of course the working classes were a much smaller part of the anti-business coalition that they were during the New Deal. But none of these facts, it seems to me, affects the main thesis of the *Age of Jackson* that more can be understood about Jacksonian Democracy if it is regarded as a problem not of sections but of classes and that liberalism in America has been ordinarily the movement on the part of the other sections of society to restrain the power of the business community."[11]

Robert T. Bower of American University questioned the validity of Pessen's interpretation of Boston electoral statistics. Bower pointed out that Pessen's data clearly indicated that, though Jackson seldom carried any wards in Whig Boston, his vote percentage in the poorer wards consistently exceeded his strength in the more prosperous parts of the city by an appreciable margin. A correct interpretation of this evidence, Bower argued, would suggest that class considerations actually did clearly influence the Boston labor vote. Joseph G. Rayback of Pennsylvania State University, in a book review published in the *Mississippi Valley Historical Review,* was equally critical of Sullivan's use of Philadelphia electoral statistics. Sullivan, he suggested, may well have been misled by the assumption that lower-class areas in Philadelphia could be pinpointed by use of property assessment data. "Value of real estate," he wrote, "is often very high in workingmen's wards by reason of the existence of industrial and commercial properties in them." To

---

Philadelphia Workingmen's Movement," *The Pennsylvania Magazine of History and Biography*, LXXVI, 142-76. Arky's findings agreed with Pessen's contention that the Workingmen regarded the Jacksonian party with distrust. 164-74.

11. "To the Editor of the American Historical Review," *American Historical Review*, LIV, 785-86.

further support his charge that Sullivan's analysis was, at best, highly inconclusive, Rayback also suggested that "the decline of the Jackson vote in the major industrial centers, moreover, may have been caused by population shifts—extensive in the 1830's—and by the drift of non-labor elements toward Whiggery." Finally, he found that Sullivan had ignored completely "the fact that Philadelphia county—which contained suburbs and liberties wherein large numbers of workingmen lived—remained staunchly Jacksonian throughout the period of decline." Although Dr. Rayback's brief review offered no positive suggestions concerning the correct methodological approach to the problem, it did serve to underline lack of consensus on the problem of the Jacksonian relationship to labor. Charles Grier Sellers of Princeton University, in an historiographic essay published in 1958, suggested that attempts "to demonstrate that workingmen did not vote for Jackson" had met "with questionable success."[12]

If the "urban labor" thesis, advanced by Schlesinger and his predecessors, proved increasingly controversial after 1945, the broader assumption that the movement "on the part of the other sections of society to restrain the power of the business community" provided the dynamic force underlying American party battles elicited a storm of scholarly controversy. With increasing frequency, historians during the past decade have challenged the validity of the Beard-Parrington-Schlesinger conception of class antagonism as the basic key to the understanding of the American political heritage. As an alternative, several scholars have suggested that consensus on basic middle-class values, not ideological controversy or class conflict, has characterized the American past. Richard Hofstadter of Columbia University called for "a reinterpretation of our political traditions which emphasizes the common climate of American opinion." The traditional emphasis on partisan conflict, he argued, had led to a serious distortion of the true nature of American political history. "However much at odds on specific issues, the major political traditions have shared a belief in the rights of property, the philosophy of economic individualism,

12. "Note on 'Did Labor Support Jackson?' The Boston Story," *Political Science Quarterly*, LXV, 441-44; Rayback, Review of *The Industrial Worker in Pennsylvania, 1800-1840*, by William A. Sullivan, *Mississippi Valley Historical Review*, XLIII, 311-12; Sellers, "Andrew Jackson versus the Historians," *ibid.*, XLIV, 615-34.

the value of competition; they have accepted the economic virtues of capitalist culture as necessary qualities for man. Even when some property right has been challenged—as it was by followers of Jefferson and Jackson—in the name of the rights of man or the rights of the community, the challenge, when translated into practical policy, has actually been urged on behalf of some other kind of property."[13]

Louis Hartz of Harvard University, applying this conception to the realm of political theory, concluded in his study of *The Liberal Tradition in America* that a commitment to Lockian values historically has been the dominant characteristic of the American political mind. The absence of rigid class barriers or of a stratified aristocracy, peasantry, or proletariat, the lack of a feudal tradition, in Hartz' analysis, rendered the traditional class antagonisms and ideological disputes of European politics irrelevant to the American scene. In this interpretation, little basic conflict underlies the bland political struggles of the American past.[14]

Recent Jacksonian historiography has been profoundly influenced by this new conception of "the common climate of American opinion." Hofstadter, applying this thesis to the Jackson era, argued that earlier historians had misinterpreted the meaning of Jacksonian Democracy because of their failure to realize that the movement was not only "a phase in the expansion of democracy" but also a phase "in the expansion of liberated capitalism." Far from providing any practical or ideological opposition to the business community, "in the Jackson period the democratic upsurge was closely linked to the ambitions of the small capitalist." Hartz suggested

13. Hofstadter, *The American Political Tradition* (New York, 1948), pp. v-xi. For a critical commentary upon this trend in American historiography, see John Higham, "The Cult of American Consensus: Homogenizing Our History," *Commentary*, XXVII, 100-21; William G. Carleton, "Political Aspects of the Van Buren Era," *South Atlantic Quarterly*, L, 167-85.

14. *The Liberal Tradition in America* (New York, 1955). For a critique of the Hartz interpretation of American political history, see Marvin Meyers, "Louis Hartz, The Liberal Tradition in America: An Appraisal," *Comparative Studies in Society and History*, I, 265-74; Harry V. Jaffa, "Conflicts within the Idea of the Liberal Tradition," *ibid.*, 274-78; Edward Estes, "Unitary and Pluralist Factors in Two Periods of the American Political Tradition: 1920-1932; 1932-1936." (Unpublished Ph.D. dissertation, University of Florida, 1963). Hartz' reply to some of his critics is contained in his "Comment," *Comparative Studies in Society and History*, I, 279-84. An interpretation of the American political tradition rather similar to that advanced by Hofstadter and Hartz is contained in Daniel Boorstin, *The Genius of American Politics* (Chicago, 1963).

that the customary portrayal of the party battles of the early nineteenth century as a struggle against "the aristocrats" or "the capitalists" originated in partisan polemics "excellently designed to
draw a red herring across the track of the American democrat's
own liberal capitalist character." He argued that the Age of Jackson, far from witnessing a desperate struggle between capital and
labor or between the business community and the rest of society,
was actually characterized by an almost unanimous acceptance of
both democracy and capitalism by both political parties. The
partisan bombast of the Jackson era, in his view, concealed a fundamental unanimity on values and an almost total sterility of political
thought.[15]

One scholar, writing in 1961, suggested that "the variety of conflicting interpretations of 'Jacksonian Democracy' reminds one
forcibly of the fable of the elephant and the six blind men, who
could not decide whether the beast was tusk, tail, ear, leg or side."
"With 'frontier,' 'labor,' and 'entrepreneurial' interpretations jos-
tling one another for place in the historian's kit," he concluded,
"the time has come when further progress in evaluating this complex
movement must be made through studies working 'from bottom up,'
analyzing specific aspects of Jacksonian politics on a local or re-
gional level, rather than focusing on the national capital or at-
tempting to encompass the national scene." Though earlier Jacksonian historiography tended to slight the local scene, several
monographs dealing with the impact of the Jacksonian movement
upon state politics began to make their appearance after 1945. Their
conclusions, however, far from resolving the heated debate over
the nature of the Jacksonian electorate and the meaning of the
Jacksonian appeal, sharply emphasized the complexity of the question of "Jacksonian Democracy."[16]

Paul Murray's study of *The Whig Party in Georgia* supported
the Beard-Schlesinger interpretation of the partisan controversies
of the Jackson era. The Whig party, Murray wrote, "attracted to
its ranks the majority of the conservative, property-minded businessmen of the country." The Georgia Whigs were "conservatives in

15. Hofstadter, pp. 45-67; Hartz, pp. 89-142. See also Hofstadter's article,
"William Leggett, Spokesman of Jacksonian Democracy," *Political Science
Quarterly*, LVIII, 581-94.
16. Martin Deming Lewis, review of Walter Hugins, *Jacksonian Democracy
and the Working Class*, *Mississippi Valley Historical Review*, XLVII, p. 503.

JACKSONIAN DEMOCRACY AND THE HISTORIANS

the real meaning of the word. . . . For the extreme democratic ideals of the Jackson era they had no respect and only the patience born of political necessity." Their organization was "an integral part of the great national organization representing the interests of business and property." Its greatest strength was centered in "those counties where cotton growing and attendant activities were dominant interests" and in "those counties where investment in primary types of manufacturing and commercial ventures supplemented cotton growing." The party battle in Jacksonian Georgia, Murray concluded, was waged between a "numerous democracy" and a party determined to "keep the government safe for the property interests."[17]

William S. Hoffman's *Andrew Jackson and North Carolina Politics*, published a decade after Murray's study, reached rather different conclusions. Hoffman, by implication, found most of the customary interpretations of Jacksonian Democracy somewhat inapplicable to the North Carolina scene. He found no evidence to indicate that the Jacksonian movement in that state was an expression of the frontier, or that the larger slaveholders opposed Old Hickory. "The greatest Democratic strength in North Carolina," he wrote, "was in the North-Central counties and in the East. Although in 1824 Jacksonism had been primarily a Western movement, by 1834 most of the important Democratic leaders were Easterners, and the personal influence of these leaders helped the party retain its Eastern majority. Generally, the districts where slavery was most prominent were safely Democratic. . . . The greatest strength of the Whigs was in the West." Party battles in North Carolina, he concluded, were not a reflection of any broad crusade for social justice or for freedom of enterprise. Of the controversy over the Bank recharter question, Hoffman wrote: "In no political quarrel was the personality of Jackson so deeply imbedded as in his war against the United States Bank. In North Carolina there was comparatively little feeling that the war on the Bank represented the common man's striving to overthrow an entrenched monopoly, the working man's desire to obtain hard money, or an attempt of the liberal capitalist to gain economic equality. Democrats tried to make the Bank war a quarrel between the people's hero and a Philadelphia banker."[18]

17. *The Whig Party in Georgia, 1825-1853* (Chapel Hill, 1948), pp. 1-3, 177-206.

18. *Andrew Jackson and North Carolina Politics* (Chapel Hill, 1958),

Hoffman also concluded that the Whigs, not the Jacksonians, anticipated the "federal aid projects sponsored by the New Deal, the Fair Deal, and the Modern Republicanism of today." In summarizing his findings concerning the two political parties in Jacksonian North Carolina, Hoffman declared: "The Democrats, on the whole, were honest men with a true devotion to principles that they rather consistently followed. They were partisan, but not as partisan as their rivals. The Whigs, generally speaking, were either consistent nationalists or self-seeking opportunists. Most of the party leaders were inconsistent and highly ambitious politicians. They were more underhanded than their rivals. Yet the policies of their party would have served the people better than the limited government concepts of their rivals. The Democrats were honest men who did little good; the Whigs were ambitious schemers whose policies would have been best for the country."[19]

Edwin A. Miles of the University of Houston found the usual explanations of the Jacksonian movement without much relevance to the Jacksonian party in Mississippi. The personal popularity of Andrew Jackson, he concluded, overshadowed all rational social or economic cleavages in explaining Mississippi politics during the Jacksonian years. "It would be fallacious to search for economic motives that might have prompted [Jackson's followers] to support particular measures endorsed by his national administration; they championed the Old Hero more often in spite of his policies rather than because of them. . . . The state Jacksonian leaders were essentially practical politicians who had hitched their wagon to Old Hickory's star and realized that their personal advancement depended upon their unequivocal support of him in all controversies." If any single factor explained their Jacksonian partisanship, Miles implied that it was, in all probability, opportunism.[20]

By contrast, Herbert J. Doherty's study of *The Whigs of Florida* found both the class cleavages and the doctrinal differences between the two parties in that state clearly discernible. Drawing upon an impressive mass of statistical data relating to election returns, slaveholding, land valuation, and crop production, Doherty concluded that the traditional findings concerning the class basis of Southern

pp. 115-22.
19. *Ibid.*, pp. 100-101, 120-22.
20. Miles, *Jacksonian Democracy in Mississippi* (Chapel Hill, 1960), pp. 168-69.

Whiggery were essentially correct. During the Jackson era, "the main appeal of the Whig party," he wrote, "was to the propertied and commercial interests, their dependent classes, and those under their influence." Whig strength was centered in the more prosperous, populous counties which led the state in "value of farm land, number of bales of cotton produced, number of slaves and size of white population." Whig officeholders in Florida, moreover, generally owned "a few more slaves and considerably more land than did their democratic colleagues." On the other hand, the "strongholds of the Democratic party in Florida were for the most part the thinly populated poorer counties which usually had more whites than slaves."[21]

Doherty warned, however, against overstating the sharpness of class cleavages in Jacksonian politics. He noted that "planters and great slaveholders and men of wealth were to be found in both parties," that "no major party in American history has ever been exclusively based on the support of, or an appeal to, the interests of an 'upper' or a 'lower' class," and that in Florida, as in America generally, both parties "appealed to and drew strength from the all pervading middle class." He argued, however, that while emphasis upon the similarities between American political parties "may be a needed corrective to the hasty tendency of survey histories and the oversimplifiers to identify parties exclusively as parties of the 'common man' or of the businessman or of farmers or of laborers," that emphasis should not be allowed to blur the very real differences, the "clear cut and often sharply conflicting desires" that have also characterized our history. Doherty found those differences definable in the late Jackson period in Florida, not only in terms of the composition of the leadership and electoral following of the two parties, but also in terms of their conflicting doctrinal viewpoint. "The Whigs" he wrote, "were more concerned with material progress and national unity and were less concerned with political democracy and the rights of man than were the Democrats. The Whigs also tended to reflect a 'status quo' outlook which established vested interests might be expected to do, while the Democrats reflected a greater sense of fluidity and change, which newcomers and younger men 'on the make' might be expected to do."[22]

21. The Whigs of Florida (Gainesville, 1959), pp. 29, 63-72.
22. Ibid., pp. 71-72. Charles Grier Sellers, in his provocative article "Who Were the Southern Whigs?" American Historical Review, LIX, 335-46, argued

Arthur W. Thompson's monograph *Jacksonian Democracy on the Florida Frontier* also rejected the thesis that the party battles of the Jacksonian era were of little meaning. "The conflicts, the emotions, the debates which were stirred up in this period," Thompson wrote, "bespeak the existence of real issues." The Jacksonian party, in Thompson's analysis, derived its strength from "the democratic temper of the age." "To Florida Democrats of the late thirties and forties," he wrote, "the democratic ideology constituted a revolt against all monopolies, political, economic or social. It challenged the power held by virtue of the opposition's 'behind-the-scenes-manipulation,' caucus nominations, inadequate appeals to the electorate, and 'government by clique.' It condemned economic privilege created by legislative grants of exclusive charters, as well as intimate connections between government and an economic elite. And it opposed the social aristocracy which had emerged in earlier territorial days. The appeal, then, was for an order devoid of any kind of special privilege."[23]

After a careful, statistical analysis of the composition of the Jacksonian leadership, Thompson found that "in many ways they were a diverse lot, more so perhaps than the Whig leaders. They included in their ranks a few large, irate, anti-bank planters, a larger number of insecure small planters; an expanding group of struggling businessmen; a number of forthright yeoman farmers, a

---

that the Southern Whigs were actually more of a businessman's party and less a party of the planter than earlier historiography had realized. His interpretation of the commercial nature of the party was based upon an analysis of Southern Whig voting behavior in Congress. See also Seller's excellent *James K. Polk, Jacksonian* (Princeton, 1957), p. 303. Grady McWhiney, in his article "Were the Whigs a Class Party in Alabama?" *Journal of Southern History*, XXIII, 510-22, questions the validity of the assumption that Southern Whig support came exclusively from large planters and businessmen.

23. *Jacksonian Democracy on the Florida Frontier* (Gainesville, 1961), pp. 23, 54-57. Thompson also found, interestingly enough, that Florida Jacksonians were not in the habit of involving Old Hickory's name in justification of their cause. "For these latter day Florida Democrats of the "Age of Jackson,' the hero was not yet the great political symbol he would become later. Rather, it was to Mr. Jefferson that these men turned. His critique of aristocracy, banking institutions and 'monied corporations' struck a responsive chord; his defense of the yeomen became part of their cause and his enemies became theirs. . . . In all the literature on the Florida Democratic movement between 1833 and 1845 Andrew Jackson is rarely, if ever, mentioned." Thompson suggested that local political factors—in particular, the tendency of Jackson's early cohorts and followers to align themselves with the Jacksonian opposition—may explain that neglect. P. 57.

considerable contingent of eager professional persons, and a small core of shrewd political entrepreneurs. Each group had its own problem and each individual had his own aspirations." The supporters of the Jacksonian movement in Florida, however, were not without a certain unity of purpose. Regardless of their differences, Thompson wrote, "most of them were alike in that they were all enterprising young men 'on the make.' They all shared common resentment against the existing order, and were determined to alter some, but by no means all, aspects of the status quo." Thompson concluded that "it may be stated with a reasonable degree of certainty that the Democratic revolt was primarily a middle class movement—middle class in the nineteenth century sense of that term—of the lesser, independent property-holding groups. And, contrary to Whig apprehensions, it was certainly no lower class manifestation of radicalism. Rather . . . it was almost exclusively a struggle to broaden the base of economic and political opportunity."[24]

Charles McColl Snyder's monograph *The Jacksonian Heritage: Pennsylvania Politics, 1838-1848* offers some verification of the conclusions reached by earlier scholars, who found evidence of class alignments in the Pennsylvania electorate during the Jacksonian era. However, Snyder's study did not offer a clear-cut interpretation of the basic nature of the Jacksonian movement. Rather, he carefully delineated the policy disputes and factional feuds which often divided the Pennsylvania Jacksonian camp against itself. Though Snyder concluded that the Jacksonian party owed their long ascendency in the Keystone State to "their success in identifying themselves with the 'will of the people,' " he found little unity or agreement in their position on such vital issues as banking policy, the tariff, or, surprisingly, even the question of democratizing the state's constitution. The powerful influence of pro-Bank and pro-tariff interests made difficult the reconciliation of the local and national Democratic parties, just as the lack of sectional unity within in the state itself contributed to the disunity within the Jacksonian organization. Snyder's carefully documented and detailed portrayal of the tangled skein of Pennsylvania politics suggested that dissension and disunity may well have been the basic characteristic of the Jacksonian movement in that state.[25]

24. *Ibid.*, pp. 58-65.
25. *The Jacksonian Heritage: Pennsylvania Politics, 1833-1848* (Harrisburg,

A few specialized studies of the Jacksonian era challenged the long-held premise that Andrew Jackson's appearance on the national political scene heralded a "great popular upheaval." Harry R. Stevens, a professor of history at Ohio State University, concluded in his investigation of *The Early Jackson Party in Ohio* that, at the beginning of the Jackson era at least, there was "very little difference between one party and another." Limiting his investigation to the election of 1824, on the rather controversial assumption that the beginnings of modern two-party divisions can be dated from that year, Stevens made an exhaustive study of the background and social position of some twelve hundred known supporters of the three major candidates in the presidential contest in that state. He found very little evidence of any division in terms of economic interests, ethnic origins, or geographical sections. The supporters of each candidate apparently comprised a cross section of the state as a whole. Finding the traditional explanations of voting behavior of little assistance, Stevens borrowed a page from the psychologists and suggested that only recourse to the irrational could explain Ohio political preferences in 1824. "Again and again," he declared, "it would seem from the nature of a man's career and from such other evidence as may throw light on his personality that men with a given outlook on life might be inclined to favor one presidential candidate rather than another. The more energetic and overtly aggressive might prefer Jackson, the more judicious and reflective, Adams, the more skilled in wire-pulling, Clay."[26]

The statistical studies of voting during the Jacksonian era published by Richard P. McCormick of Rutgers University also questioned the validity of the customary concept of a Jacksonian popular revolution. In an analysis of "Suffrage Classes and Party Alignments," published in the *Mississippi Valley Historical Review*, McCormick reported that a study of election returns in North Carolina, which had a system of dual suffrage requiring property holding in elections for some offices, but not others, offered little evidence of any relationship between economic status and voter behavior. In a subsequent article in the *American Historical Review*, McCormick challenged the widely held thesis that Andrew Jackson's elevation

---

1958), pp. 22-49, 82-95, 99-101, 112-35.
  26. *The Early Jackson Party in Ohio* (Durham, 1957), pp. v-vi, 148-49, 151, 160.

to the Presidency in 1828 represented a mass upheaval of democracy. Mass participation in elections, he argued, did not occur until *after* Old Hickory's retirement from political life. During Jackson's presidency, most voters generally either stayed home on election day or evinced more interest in state and local contests than in national campaigns.[27]

Perhaps the most comprehensive—and provocative—challenge to the customary interpretations of "Jacksonian Democracy" was provided, however, by Professor Lee Benson. In a survey of voting behavior and political rhetoric in New York during the Jacksonian era (with particular emphasis upon the election of 1844) Benson suggested that "the concept of Jacksonian Democracy has obscured rather than illuminated" the course of New York history after 1815. Preoccupation with this misleading abstraction, he submitted, "has distracted historians from the significance of their own work, and has led them to offer interpretations that are contradicted by their own findings." Benson argued further than "since events in New York are invariably cited by historians who accept some version of the concept, systematic research may find that in other states the concept also does not conform to reality."[28]

In testing the validity of "the concept of Jacksonian Democracy," Benson turned first to the assumption that "the party formulated and fought for an egalitarian ideology that envisioned not only political but social and economic democracy." After investigating both the legislative history of New York and the official programs and unofficial pronouncements of both parties during the Jackson era, he found that the Jacksonian party "attacked rather than sponsored the Whig idea of the positive liberal state functioning to 'equalize the condition of men.' . . . Instead of vigorously implementing, it uncompromisingly opposed political programs that required the state to act positively to foster democratic egalitarianism, economic democracy, social and humanitarian reform." The Jacksonians, Benson concluded, "expressed a particular ideology and implemented a program consonant with it, but its ideology and program derived from the old doctrines of states rights, strong

27. "Suffrage Classes and Party Alignments: A Study in Voter Behavior," *Mississippi Valley Historical Review*, XLVI, 399-410; "New Perspectives on Jacksonian Politics," *American Historical Review*, XLV, 288-301.
28. Benson, *The Concept of Jacksonian Democracy: New York as a Test Case* (Princeton, 1961), pp. 332-35.

executive, freedom of conscience, and the new doctrine of negative government." In obvious reference to the Schlesinger interpretation of Jacksonian Democracy, Benson suggested that "the Whigs come closer than the Democrats in satisfying the requirements of historians in search of nineteenth-century precursors to twentieth-century New Dealers."[29]

Benson also found the Dorfman interpretation of the Jacksonian movement as an expression of middle-class demands for freedom of enterprise somewhat inapplicable to New York politics. Pointing to the close involvement of the state-chartered banking interests with the Albany Regency, and to the hostility between the regular democratic organization and the pro-laissez-faire Workingmen's groups, he argued that the Jacksonian leaders in New York, far from leading the antimonopoly movement, "were its targets." Only reluctantly did the Regency finally come to embrace the Locofoco laissez faire philosophy.[30]

New York politics during the Jackson era, in Benson's view, could not be portrayed, with any accuracy, as a conflict between liberal and conservative parties. Rather, endorsing the Hofstadter-Hartz thesis of liberal consensus as the basic characteristic of the American political tradition, he concluded that "despite their clashes over the positive state, locus of government power, role of different government branches, and foreign policy, both the Demo-

29. *Ibid*, pp. 3-63, 86-109, 331-32. In substantiating this contention, Benson pointed out that, contrary to the assumption that the Jacksonians spear-headed the drive for universal suffrage, the followers of Van Buren, the nucleus of the future New York Jacksonian party, opposed both demands for the popular election of presidential electors and for elimination of all voter property qualifications. Though "the Van Buren faction and then the Jackson party eventually capitulated and adopted the egalitarian ideology advocated by their [anti-Masonic] opponents," the New York Jacksonians, Benson submitted, "resolutely resisted social reform in New York." In 1830 their platform "ignored demands for abolition of licensed monopolies, abolition of imprisonment for debt, and establishment of a system of equal education for all." Later, they denounced the supporters of the Workingmen's party, a reformist organization, as the advocates of "doctrines that 'strike at the very roots of established morals and good order of society.'" Though their anti-Masonic opponents crusaded for the abolition of imprisonment for debt, Benson found the New York Jacksonians "divided on it and yielded only to the rising tide of popular feeling." Though the Whigs frequently supported legislative measures designed to provide state aid for the support of public education or for the relief of paupers and orphans, Jacksonians, in Benson's analysis, were devoted to the ideology of the "negative liberal state", and they usually opposed all such legislation.

30. *Ibid.*, pp. 47-49.

crats and the Whigs stood firmly committed to political democracy (for white men) and to liberal capitalism."[31]

Benson found the concept of Jacksonian Democracy as the expression of lower-class farm-labor grievances as inapplicable to the New York scene as the portrayal of the Jacksonian movement as the vanguard of liberal reformism. Statistical evidence, he argued, offers little support to the view that poorer farmers and laborers were solidly Jacksonian and the more affluent farmers, businessmen, and manufacturers, Whig. After analyzing the social background and economic status of the leaders of both parties, he concluded that "neither Schlesinger's version, nor any other version that assumes there were significant differences in the class nature of party leadership appears credible. Instead, the evidence indicates that the same socioeconomic groups provided leadership for both parties." After analyzing the election returns, Benson also found no correlation between per capita wealth and a town's voting behavior. The data failed to yield any evidence of a rural-urban division in partisan loyalties, either. As to the assertion that the wealthy tended to oppose Jackson, Benson, checking party endorsements against a guide to "The Wealth and Biography of Wealthy Citizens of New York," published in 1845, found no appreciable difference in the identifiable political preferences of the very affluent. He also found, in contemporary newspaper accounts, evidence that "a large proportion of the capitalists, landlords, bankers, and brokers" supported the Jacksonian cause.[32]

Benson suggested that historians who had assumed the existence of such divisions had been badly misled by Martin Van Buren's assertion, in his history of American political parties, that class antagonisms underlie Jacksonian politics. "The evidence," Benson wrote, "discredits his claims that the Jackson party championed the 'producers' against the 'special interests.' According to his persuasive rhetoric, the Jacksonians took the side of the producers in the conflict between 'those who live by the sweat of their brow and those who live by their wits.' When we penetrated the rhetorical surface and struck hard data, however, we found that farmers, mechanics and working classes did not form the 'main stay of the Democratic party.' Instead of low status socioecenomic groups, the Jacksonian's strongest support came from relatively high status socioeconomic groups in eastern counties and relatively low status

31. *Ibid.*, pp. 86-109, 216-53, 292.   32. *Ibid.*, pp. 123-64, 331.

72

ethnocultural and religious groups in all sections of New York."[33]

Rejecting the theory that the voting patterns of the Jacksonian era were primarily a reflection of socioeconomic cleavages, Benson endeavored to provide an alternative theory to explain voter motivation during the "Age of Egalitarianism." After an investigation of the voting behavior of selected towns of varying ethnocultural and religious backgrounds, Benson suggested that "at least since the 1820's, when manhood suffrage became widespread, ethnic and religious differences have tended to be relatively the most important sources of political differences." In the election of 1844, Benson found certain ethnic groups solidly, almost monolithically, democratic; others, equally Whig in their partisanship. The mutual antipathies of the groups composing the electorate (their "negative reference groups"), Benson suggested, helped explain this phenomenon. For example, Catholic immigrants resented the nativist views of many Whigs, non-Catholic immigrants distrusted the Papist convictions of many Democrats; Negroes were alienated by the anti-Negro bigotry of many Democratic spokesmen. "The stand of the major parties on socioeconomic issues," he concluded, "had little effect upon block voting in New York."[34]

Ethnocultural and religious factors *alone* did not fully explain Jacksonian voting behavior in Benson's analysis, however. Native Protestants, he found, did not vote in a solid block but tended to divide between the two parties. A variety of determinants, Benson suggested, influenced their vote: local traditions; local economic conditions; negative reference groups (the antagonism of the Dutch Democrat and the Yankee Whig, for example); or their attitude toward puritanism (the Jacksonian party's image was antipuritan), the Negro (the Jacksonians were anti-Negro), or the nativist (the Jacksonians were also antinativist). Benson called for the development of techniques of "multi-variate analysis" capable of taking into account the many different determinants of voting behavior. He criticized the economic determinists for their reliance on one factor alone, but did not reject altogether the possibility of a relationship "between economic class and voting during the 1830's and 1840's."[35]

Though the monographic studies of state politics during the

---

33. *Ibid.*, pp. 288-328, 331-32. 34. *Ibid.*, pp. 166-90.
35. *Ibid.*, pp. 191-207, 270-87. Benson suggested that a theory of American

Jacksonian era were divided in their evaluations of the nature of Jacksonian democracy, two rather unique specialized investigations of Jacksonian rhetoric published in the late 1950's agreed in finding the roots of the Jacksonian appeal in the intense anxieties of those who feared social change and held the good life possible only in an agrarian, frontier society. John W. Ward of Princeton University, in his *Andrew Jackson: Symbol for an Age*, sought to determine what meaning the image of Old Hickory held for those who voted for Jackson. After a detailed study of the partisan campaign literature of the Jacksonian movement, Ward concluded that, to his supporters, Andrew Jackson personified belief in the agrarian ideal, rejection of the influence of Europe, distrust of the intellectual, faith in the untutored, intuitive mind, fervent confidence in the divine sanction of the American mission, as well as "the ideal of self-sufficient individualism which was the inevitable rationalization of America's disorganized development."[36]

In a sense, Ward suggested, the Jacksonian appeal was reactionary, not progressive. "The image of Jackson apparently accepted by a majority of the people," he wrote, ". . . rejected a complete acceptance of the advanced stages of civilization. This ambivalent attitude was possible as long as the United States fronted free land so that its progress in civilization was constantly regenerated by contact with nature. The solution of a periodic return to nature was an uneasy one, however, since it had an obvious temporal limit. What was more important, the ideal of the admixture of nature and civilization was a static one. It could be achieved only in the pioneer stage when the wilderness had been subdued but the enervating influence of civilization had not yet been felt. As America moved toward a denser civilization, the conflict in logic implicit in the two ideas made ideological adjustment to a new social stage difficult. Jacksonian democratic thought, built upon a philosophy of nature in the concrete, was oriented toward a period in American social development that was slipping away at the very moment of its formulation."[37]

---

voting behavior might be constructed based upon analysis of the following main categories of determinants: 1) Pursuit of political goals by individuals or groups, 2) individual or group fulfillment of political roles, 3) negative or positive orientation to reference individuals or groups. P. 281.

36. *Andrew Jackson, Symbol for an Age* (New York, 1955). Ward acknowledged in his introduction a profound indebtedness to Henry Nash Smith, whose provocative *Virgin Land* appeared in 1950. 37. *Ibid.*, p. 45.

In *The Jacksonian Persuasion,* Marvin Meyers of the University of Chicago sought to probe the psychological basis of the Jacksonian political appeal. Through an analysis of Jacksonian rhetoric combined with a careful reading of de Tocqueville, Cooper, and other contemporary observers and participants, he endeavored to isolate the "fears and hopes, the passions and beliefs that underlay . . . party loyalty" during the Age of Jackson. Meyers concluded that the followers of Old Hickory played upon "the diffuse fears and resentments" of Americans living in an age of bewildering social and economic change. Their Whig opponents, on the other hand, "spoke to [their] explicit hopes." The Jacksonians, in his interpretation, looked to the past, the Whigs to the future.[38]

Jacksonian Democracy, Meyers argued, gave expression to the guilt and anxieties of men who, though pursuing the capitalist dream of wealth, with bucolic nostalgia longed for the simple, virtuous agrarian society of the past. Restoration of the "Old Republic" of Jefferson, not the creation of a new democratic society, was the essence of the Jacksonian conception of their historical mission. "Jacksonian Democracy," Meyers wrote, "sought to recall agrarian republican innocence to a society drawn fatally to the main chance and the long chance, to revolutionizing ways of acquisition, emulative consumption, promotion and speculation." It was foredoomed to failure, for "the generation that voted for Jackson and the restoration of old republican virture was as acquisitive and speculative as any in American history." Pointing to the involvement of many Jacksonians in the very type of speculative ventures their rhetoric denounced, Meyers declared the followers of Old Hickory "both the judges and the judged."[39]

Meyers' treatment of Jacksonian Democracy contrasted sharply with the pro-Jacksonian partisanship characteristic of earlier twentieth-century historiography. In most respects his judgment of the merits of the Jacksonian cause was a harsh one. He found their

38. *The Jacksonian Persuasion* (New York, 1960), pp. v-ix, 3-16. Meyers' work first appeared in 1957. The citations here are from the Vintage paperback edition of three years later. See also Meyers' articles "The Great Descent: A Version of Fenimore Cooper," *The Pacific Spectator,* X, 367-81; "The Jacksonian Persuasion," *American Quarterly,* V, 3-15.

39. *Ibid.,* pp. 10-15, 21-24, 31-52, 74-77, 191-93, 212-22. Unlike Dorfman, Meyers did not regard the Jacksonians as conscious advocates of liberal capitalism. Though the Jacksonians invoked laissez faire and sought to unfetter enterprise, they were, in his judgment, without a vision of the future. He found that though the Jacksonian program, viewed from the perspective of the present,

intellectual appeal superficial and limited, and labelled Old Hickory's presidential messages "ragged political philosophy, tendentious accounting, crude policy." He pronounced the anxieties expressed in Jacksonian rhetoric quite absurd. Writing of the Bank war, Meyers declared: "Broad popular hatred and fear of the Second Bank, invoked by the Jacksonian appeals, cannot be understood simply as a matter of fact reaction to material injuries. The economic operations of the institution conferred some manifest general benefits, directly crossed the interests of only a limited group; its hand was not upon men's throats or in their pockets." He found the Jacksonian fear of speculation shortsighted and unrealistic. Though granting that many of the speculative ventures of Jackson's day proved disastrous to the economy in the short run, Meyers argued that the "basic sense of direction" of the speculator provided the "key to . . . creative economic development." The Whigs in appealing to the great optimism of Americans in the Age of Jackson, Meyers concluded, spoke from a justifiable confidence in the nation's future, while the Jacksonians were imprisoned by their fears and looked only to the past.[40]

Glyndon G. Van Deusen of the University of Rochester, author of *The New American Nation Series* volume on the Jacksonian era and biographer of Clay, Greeley, and Weed, also found the Jacksonian program hopelessly out of touch with the needs of an expanding capitalist society. The Jacksonian movement, Ven Deusen declared, was "so heavily imbued with archaic notions about corporations, currency, and do-nothing government, that it would sooner or later have gone down to defeat, even without the aid of the great depression of 1837 it helped to bring on." The destruction of the Bank of the United States, in Van Deusen's analysis, reflected this outmoded economic philosophy. Through this short-sighted act, the followers of Old Hickory "fostered speculation," struck a "blow to the development of a sound credit policy and contributed

---

"ought to appeal to the interests of one particular group, ambitious new business enterprises," in actual fact the Jacksonian message "barely acknowledges its logical beneficiaries, often abuses their traits and ways, and unmistakably favored other social types whose economic interests could be promoted only negatively and indirectly by such messages."

40. *Ibid.*, pp. 10, 17, 31, 101-4. In his interpretation of the speculative mania of the Jackson era, Meyers drew heavily on Joseph A. Schumpeter, *Business Cycles* (New York, 1939), I, 294-96, as well as on the students of banking cited later in this chapter.

materially to the currency chaos that characterized the succeeding decades." Though Van Deusen praised the Jacksonians' interest in preserving equality of economic opportunity" and "devotion to the rights of the common man," he argued that their economic program was actually less progressive than that offered by the Whig opposition. Rejecting the Schlesinger interpretation of the Jacksonian movement as the precursor of twentieth-century liberalism, Van Deusen concluded that "the Whig attitude toward the role of government, on the national level, bears a closer resemblance to that of the New Deal than did the attitude toward government of Jackson and Van Buren." He added, however, that "the political conflicts of the Jackson period were fought more often with a view of gaining control of the government than out of devotion to diametrically opposed political and social ideals."[41]

Charles M. Wiltse's massive biography of John C. Calhoun, published in three volumes between 1944 and 1951, provided further support to those who deprecated the pro-Jacksonian partisanship of Schlesinger and his followers. No admirer of Old Hickory, Wiltse portrayed Andrew Jackson as a "frontier bully" and, borrowing a phrase from William Wirt, dismissed the political ascendancy of his followers as the "millennium of the minnows." Unlike many critics of the Schlesinger interpretation, however, Wiltse did not completely reject the thesis that class antagonisms provided the key to understanding the Jacksonian movement. Indeed, he found the "proletariat" the sustaining force behind Jackson's political power.[42]

41. Van Deusen, "Some Aspects of Whig Thought and Theory in the Jacksonian Period," *American Historical Review*, LX, 305-22; *The Jacksonian Era, 1828-1848* (New York, 1959), XV-XVI, 26-131. See also Van Deusen's *Henry Clay* (Boston, 1937), *Thurlow Weed, Wizard of the Lobby*, (Boston, 1947), and *Horace Greeley, Nineteenth Century Crusader*, (Philadelphia, 1953).

42. *John C. Calhoun, Nationalist* (Indianapolis, 1944), p. 271; *John C. Calhoun, Nullifier* (Indianapolis, 1949), pp. 11-25, 154-56. See also Wiltse's *The New Nation* (New York, 1961), pp. 91-155. Unfortunately space limitations preclude treatment of several other excellent biographies of leading figures of the Jacksonian era published during the last decade and a half. Note should be made, however, of Margaret L. Coit, *John C. Calhoun: American Portrait* (Boston, 1950); Charles Grier Sellers, *James K. Polk, Jacksonian* (Princeton, 1957); Elbert B. Smith, *Magnificent Missourian: The Life of Thomas Hart Benton* (Philadelphia, 1958); Samuel Flagg Bemis, *John Quincy Adams and the Union* (New York, 1956); William Nesbit Chambers, *Old Bullion Benton* (Boston, 1956); Richard N. Current, *Daniel Webster and the Rise of National Conservatism* (Boston, 1955); Clement Eaton, *Henry Clay and the Art of American Politics* (Boston, 1957); John A. Garraty, *Silas Wright* (New York,

Wiltse's heated castigation of the Jacksonians rested partly upon the contention, advanced a century before by George Tucker, that the cohorts of Old Hickory were without any consistent, statesman-like political philosophy but relied upon the demagogic manipulation of the unthinking masses to sustain their political power. Taking issue with Schlesinger, he wrote: "It does not seem to me to be possible to fit either the actions or the professions of Jackson's two terms of office into any kind of pattern save that of opportunism, and of give and take between forces battling for the upper hand." Wiltse deplored the ruthlessness, corruption, and unprincipled demagogery which, in his view, pervaded the Jacksonian party. In language rather reminiscent of Gilded Age protests against the Jacksonian degradation of the Republic, he lamented the eclipse of statesmanship which followed in the wake of Jackson's elevation to the Presidency.[43]

His rejection of Jacksonian Democracy was grounded in more than mere distaste for Old Hickory and his followers, however. Identifying closely with the subject of his biography, Wiltse lauded Calhoun as the philosophical defender of the "rights of minorities everywhere" and sympathized with the South Carolina stateman's efforts to erect conservative safeguards against the potential tyranny of the majority. Andrew Jackson, on the other hand, symbolized to Wiltse the naked force of majority rule unrestrained by constitutional scruples. Of the Nullification Proclamation, he declared: "In four short years Jackson had led his party from bitter opposition to the consolidating tendencies of John Quincy Adams to a form of authoritarianism that outdid even the Alien and Sedition Acts of Adams' father. The individualistic democracy of the frontier lost ground to the cult of power so dear to wealth and property."[44]

In recent years students of banking history have also voiced criticism of the pro-Democratic interpretation of the party battles

---

1949); W. H. Hale, *Horace Greeley* (New York, 1950); Robert V. Remini, *Martin Van Buren and the Making of the Democratic Party* (New York, 1959); Ivor D. Spencer, *The Victor and the Spoils: A Life of William L. Marcy* (Providence, R. I., 1959); Francis F. Wayland, *Andrew Stevenson, Democrat and Diplomat* (Philadelphia, 1959); Philip S. Klein, *President James Buchanan* (University Park, Pa., 1962).

43. Wiltse, *John C. Calhoun: Nullifier*, pp. 39-52, 86-97, 169-82, 419.

44. *Ibid.*, pp. 110-21, 143-53, 183-95; *John C. Calhoun Nationalist*, pp. 397-98. For a provocative corrective of the pro-Calhoun bias of most of Calhoun's

of the Jackson era. Fritz Redlich, in his monograph, *The Moulding of American Banking: Men and Ideas*, challenged the harsh treatment accorded Nicholas Biddle and the Second Bank of the United States in the writings of the Democratic school. Applying modern central banking theory to his analysis of the Jacksonian war against the Bank, Redlich lauded Biddle as a notable and creative forerunner of the twentieth-century central banker and praised the Second Bank as a useful, indeed, necessary stabilizer of the currency. His conclusions were shared by Walter B. Smith in his *Economic Aspects of the Second Bank of the United States*. Smith found that both Biddle's supporters and his opponents tended to exaggerate the economic power of the Second Bank. Nonetheless, he found the Bank's influence, on balance, a creative one. "Had the institution been allowed to develop, as it gave promise of doing," Smith wrote, "the United States would have had an effective banking system long before it did." "The benefits," he added, "would have been substantial." In Smith's interpretation, Jackson's misinformed policies severely retarded the development of an adequate banking system. "From being one of the most financially inventive countries in the world, the United States was transformed into one of the most backward in the years following the demise of the Second Bank of the United States." Both Redlich and Smith argued that the continuation of the Second Bank would have strengthened the entire economy and served the interests of all groups and social classes. Both, though mildly critical of Biddle's arrogance and lack of political tact, portrayed the Pennsylvania banker, not as a powerful, selfish, grasping monopolist, but rather as a creative economic statesman.[45]

Bray Hammond, assistant secretary of the Board of Governors of the Federal Reserve System, fully shared the misgivings expressed

---

biographers, see Gerald Capers, *John C. Calhoun: Opportunist* (Gainesville, Fla., 1962). A useful analysis of the Calhoun literature is provided in Harold B. Schultz, "A Century of Calhoun Biographies," *South Atlantic Quarterly*, L, 248-54.

45. *The Moulding of American Banking: Men and Ideas* (New York, 1947), pp. 150 ff.; *Economic Aspects of the Second Bank of the United States* (Cambridge, 1953), pp. 1-17, 116-263. Though praising Biddle's financial acumen, recent banking scholars have differentiated between Biddle's successful career as a public banker and the unfortunate period after 1836 when Biddle's institution, operating under a Pennsylvania state charter, it is generally agreed exemplified the worst vices of the banks of the period.

by Redlich and Smith concerning the anti-Biddle bias characteristic of much twentieth-century Jacksonian historiography. In his Pulitzer prize winning *Banks and Politics in America,* Hammond argued that the pro-Jacksonian view of the struggle against the Bank as "one of idealism against lucre and of human rights against property rights" badly distorted the actual objectives of the Jacksonian party. Endorsing the "entrepreneurial" interpretation of the Jacksonian movement, Hammond declared: "The Jacksonians were no less drawn by lucre than the so-called conservatives, but rather more. They had no greater concern for human rights than the people who had what they were trying to get." The desire of interested groups, particularly the state chartered banks, to profit from the destruction of Biddle's institution, in Hammond's interpretation, provided the basic motive behind the Bank war. After carefully enumerating the banking ventures and commercial speculations which involved leading members of Jackson's "Kitchen Cabinet" and numerous state leaders of the Jacksonian party, Hammond concluded that the Jacksonian cause "was a sophisticated one of enterpriser against capitalist, of banker against regulation, and of Wall Street against Chesnut."[46]

The triumph of the Jacksonians, as Hammond saw it, led not to a more democratic society but to the emergence of a new, more rapacious class of capitalist-speculators. Despite their protestations of democratic idealism, the followers of Old Hickory "made the Age of Jackson a festival of *laissez faire* precursive to the Age of Grant and the Robber Barons." "The millionaires created by the so-called Jacksonian revolution of 'agrarians' and 'capitalists,'" Hammond wrote, "were richer than those they dispossessed, they were more numerous, they were quite as ruthless; and *laissez faire,* after destroying the monopolies and vested rights the Jacksonians decried, produced far greater ones." Hammond not only praised

46. *Banks and Politics in America* (Princeton, 1957), pp. vii-x, 326-450. See also Hammond's earlier articles, "Jackson, Biddle and the Bank of the United States," *Journal of Economic History*, VII, 1-23; "Banking in the Early West: Monopoly, Prohibition and Laissez-Faire," *ibid.*, VIII, 1-25; "Free Banking and Corporations: The New York Free Banking Act of 1838," *Journal of Political Economy*, XLIV, 189-209. In his earlier writings, Hammond placed slightly less emphasis upon the entrepreneurial interpretation of the Jacksonian movement, and paid somewhat more attention to the "hard money" left-wing faction of the Democratic party than in his *Banks and Politics* which focused primarily, though not exclusively, upon the role of the state banks in the Jacksonian crusade.

the operations of the Bank of the United States as a needed stabilizing and regulating force; he also portrayed the struggle of Nicholas Biddle versus the Jacksonians as the struggle of an old, cultured commercial aristocracy against a new, grasping class of commercial adventurers concerned only with self-aggrandisement. The democratic impulses of the Jackson era, in Hammond's view, led not to the liberal idealism of the New Deal, but to the sordid cynicism of the Age of Grant.[47]

A very similar interpretation of the issues at stake in the Bank war was voiced in Thomas P. Govan's biography of Nicholas Biddle, published in 1959. Govan lauded the Bank as a useful institution whose operations benefited all classes, and condemned the presumed ignorance and irresponsibility of the Jacksonian politician. "Jackson, Benton, Gouge and Woodbury and their associates," Govan argued, "could never understand that the various economic groups were mutually dependent on one another and the prosperity of one contingent on that of the others. They looked with suspicion upon merchants, manufacturers, bankers, and financiers and assumed that the interests of these groups could be adversely influenced without destroying the market for the produce of the farmers or creating unemployment for the workers." Govan unlike Hammond, did not endorse the findings of the entrepreneurial school; in his interpretation anticapitalist prejudice, vicious and irresponsible, shaped the crusade against the Bank. He did join, however, with those who challenged the relevance of the Jacksonian heritage to twentieth-century liberalism. Drawing a parallel with the New Deal, Govan found that many of the policies employed by Franklin D. Roosevelt "to overcome a depression were essentially identical with those that had been advocated and followed almost a century before by Biddle, a banker and a Hamiltonian nationalist, in a similar economic situation."[48]

47. *Banks and Politics*, pp. 326-450.
48. Govan, *Nicholas Biddle, Nationalist and Public Banker* (Chicago, 1959), pp. vii, 300, 304. Govan's biography is rather unique in that, unlike other scholars such as Redlich, Smith, and Hammond who have regarded Biddle as a poor politician, Govan attributed the Philadelphia bankers' political failure in the recharter controversy solely to the harshness of fate. He found some evidence that Biddle did use public funds to enlist others in the Bank's cause, but added "he was willing to bribe, not to increase his personal power or wealth," but to serve the public which "needed an institution such as the United States Bank." "The morality of his action," Govan concluded, "is a question not easy to solve."

81

The revisionist interpretation of the Bank controversy has not, however, won the unanimous support of Jacksonian scholars. The eminent economic historian, George Rogers Taylor, in his study of *The Transportation Revolution*, argued that Biddle's institution was in no sense "a responsible central bank." The lack of adequate public control over the policies of the Bank, combined with the ever-present danger of overissuance of the bank notes, in Taylor's mind, gave ample justification to the Jacksonian opposition to recharter. "Because the abuses of uncontrolled state banking became notorious, or because the second Bank of the United States operated at times *somewhat like* a modern central bank," Taylor wrote, "it does not follow that Biddle's bank should have been rechartered." Leonard D. White, the noted student of public administration, concurred. Though noting that the Bank's public services were "well performed," White, in his book *The Jacksonians: A Study in Administrative History*, held that "the underlying problem was the lack of effective governmental control over the financial power of the bank, and the inherent conflict between the economic power of the Bank, personified in Nicholas Biddle, and the political power of the government, personified in Andrew Jackson." In their evaluations of the Jacksonian campaign against the Bank of the United States, as in many other aspects of the turbulent and confusing Age of Jackson, historians as yet have not arrived at a common consensus in their interpretations and judgments.[49]

Over a century has now elapsed since the publication of George Tucker's pioneering narrative of the Jacksonian era, but that scholar's lament on the lack of consensus concerning Andrew Jackson and the political movement he led has lost little of its original validity. Tucker wrote: "General Jackson, of all men who have acted the chief parts in the great political theatre, has excited the most discordant sentiments of his countrymen, not excluding Mr. Jefferson. While he has been eulogized by one party as a second Washington, and by even a few as Washington's superior, he has been denied by most of the other party any one virtue but courage and decision and has been pronounced wanting in all the essential requirements of statesmanship and civic duty." The profound disagreement which Tucker noted in his countrymen's evaluations of Old Hickory now extends to every aspect of the Jacksonian period.

49. *The Transportation Revolution* (New York, 1951), pp. 310-11; *The Jacksonians: A study in Administrative History* (New York, 1954), pp. 463-75.

The debate over the meaning of Jacksonian Democracy continues and, if anything, grows more heated with the passage of years. Historians have been unable to agree either in their efforts to analyze, objectively, the nature and origins of the Jacksonian party or in their inevitably less objective evaluations of the Jacksonian contribution to the American political heritage. A reading of Jacksonian historiography tends to disabuse one of the existence of "the judgment of history." History has sustained neither the partisans nor the foes of Old Hickory, for historians cannot agree upon a verdict.

One possible explanation for this lack of consensus over the years can be found in the tendency of each scholarly generation to reinterpret the Jacksonian era in terms of its own contemporary frame of reference. A pronounced degree of "presentism"—the interpretation and judgment of the past in terms of the conditions and values of the present—has always characterized the historiography of Jacksonian Democracy.

Gilded Age scholars, for example, were preoccupied with the more sordid aspects of the spoils system democracy of their own day and were deeply alarmed by the rising tides of agrarian radicalism symbolized by the Greenback and Free Silver movements. They tended, almost without exception, to condemn the Jacksonians as the originators of most of the political abuses of their generation. As conservatives fearful of social unrest, they deplored the Jacksonian incitement of the poor against the rich. As patrician scholars oppressed by the uglier aspects of the democratic order—Grantism, Tweedism, corruption in government, the degradation of the public service—they regarded the Jacksonian era as the advent of mass democracy in all its vulgarity and judged it accordingly.

Historians of the following generation, often caught up in the Progressive crusade to revitalize democracy and check the encroachments of special privilege, saw the party battles of the Jackson era in quite a different light. If their Gilded Age predecessors granted the seal of scholarly approval to Whig polemics against spoils system politics and presidential despotism, writers of the early twentieth century were attracted to the concept of the Jacksonians as defenders of the principle of popular rule. They found Frederick Jackson Turner's interpretation of Jacksonian Democracy as an expression of the egalitarian idealism and nationalism of the American western frontier most attractive. There were several

83

reasons for the appeal of the frontier thesis. Middle-class Americans of the Progressive era were generally fearful of both the growing power of monopoly capitalism and of the threat posed by the potential radicalism of the industrial proletariat. Torn between recognition of the need to cope with the changing needs of a complex industrial society and a longing for the America of the past, for an America free of class antagonisms or industrial tensions, scholars of that generation were naturally attracted to the Turner image of the Jacksonian movement as a struggle to preserve and extend the egalitarian society of frontier America while checking the power of corporate wealth and special privilege as symbolized by the Bank of the United States. Jackson, in their narratives, came to personify the virtues of an earlier Republic, a Republic in which it was believed economic opportunity rendered class antagonisms irrelevant and a vigilant Democracy made impossible the triumph of corporate power. Perhaps because they feared the class antagonisms of their own day, these scholars placed only incidental emphasis upon the class antagonisms of the Jackson period. In the Jacksonian frontier they found their social ideal.

As the twentieth century progressed, however, the explanation of Jacksonian Democracy advanced by the agrarian democratic school appeared increasingly inadequate. Some later scholars, writing in the milieu of an urban, industrial America, found both the role of labor and the factor of class conflict of great importance in explaining our past. Moreover, in the midst of an economy characterized by boom and bust, affluence and poverty, social reform came to command growing attention as a major theme of American history. Accordingly, historians of the 1920's and 1930's placed heavy emphasis upon the importance of the Jacksonian labor movement.

During the past decade and a half, however, this interpretation has been challenged by those historians who have argued that concensus on basic middle-class values, not ideological conflict or class antagonism, has characterized our history. Some contemporary writers, regarding the Jacksonian campaign against the Bank as empty demagogery designed to advance the interests of rival entreprenurial groups jealous of the Bank's prerogatives, have concluded that no significant differences in basic objectives separated the two major parties during the Jacksonian era. Others, though recognizing the presence of business elements within the Jacksonian coalition, have stressed the reactionary nature of the Jacksonian appeal and program and denied its kinship to modern liberalism. It may be that much of the current revisionism has reflected the frame of reference of the present. This point, however, should not be unduly labored. Though historians from Tucker's day to our own have probably been influenced, in varying degrees, by the preoccupations of their generation, the Jacksonian historiography of the past few decades has evinced a higher degree of sophistication in handling source materials and a greater degree of detachment in evaluating the partisan battles of the Jackson era than was apparent in nineteenth- or even in early twentieth-century historiography. The relatively sober tone of recent works on the Jackson era compares favorably with the blatant partisanship of earlier narratives, monographs, and biographies. Their increasing sobriety no doubt reflects a higher degree of professional competence. It may also reflect the increasing irrelevance of the Jacksonian position to the partisan issues of our own day.

This heightened spirit of detachment has not, however, led to any consensus in scholarly evaluations of the nature of Jacksonian Democracy. Perhaps the fable of the blind men and the elephant may suggest one reason why. The Jacksonian movement may have been so highly pluralistic as to render impossible its definition within the framework of any single concept. In their way, the frontier democracy, urban labor, and entreprenurial theses may all be quite valid. The question may in the future resolve itself into the problem of tracing the relationships between the often conflicting, frequently contradictory elements which composed the party of Andrew Jackson. It is perhaps significant that although the last decade and a half has witnessed the appearance of numerous specialized monographs, no interpretative synthesis of the scope of Schlesinger's *Age of Jackson*, no major study of the life and times of Andrew Jackson, has made its appearance in print.

One thing is probable: the spirit of detachment, of analysis, will not in the near future lead to a complete and total objectivity in dealing with the turbulent Age of Jackson. As long as the relationship of the business community to government, of government to the citizen, and of the states to the national government remains controversial, the Jacksonian movement will be an object of controversy. The passage of time has dulled the partisan conflict of Whig versus Jacksonian; it has not totally effaced that conflict. By careful effort, the historian may minimize the distortions of the past produced by his own partisanship and by the frame of reference of the present; as a competent scholar he should struggle to do so. It is doubtful, however, that he will completely succeed.

ACKNOWLEDGMENTS

The author wishes to thank the following publishers and copyright holders for permission to quote from the indicated materials: Thomas P. Abernethy for *From Frontier to Plantation in Tennessee: A Study of Frontier Democracy*; the *American Historical Review* for articles by Darling, Dorfman, Van Deusen, and Morris; Richard Bassett for John Spencer Bassett, *Life of Andrew Jackson*; the University of Chicago Press for Thomas P. Govan, *Nicholas Biddle: Nationalist and Public Banker* (copyright, University of Chicago Press, 1959); Columbia University Press for Dixon Ryan Fox, *Decline of Aristocracy in the Politics of New York*, and Henry R. Mueller, *The Whig Party in Pennsylvania*; Duke University Press for Henry R. Stevens, *The Early Jackson Party in Ohio*; Harcourt, Brace and World for Vernon Louis Parrington, *Main Currents in American Thought*, and Louis Hartz, *The Liberal Tradition in America*; Harvard University Press for Walter B. Smith, *Economic Aspects of the Second Bank of the United States*; the Historical Society of Pennsylvania for Louis Arky, "The Mechanics Union of Trade Associations and the Formation of the Philadelphia Workingmen's Movement"; Holt, Rinehart and Winston, Inc., for William E. Dodd, *Expansion and Conflict*, and George Rogers Taylor, *The Transportation Revolution: 1815-1860*; Alfred A. Knopf for Richard Hofstadter, *The American Political Tradition*; Little, Brown and Company for Arthur M. Schlesinger, Jr., *The Age of Jackson*; Macmillan Company for Edward Channing, *History of the United States*, John R. Commons, *The History of Labour in the United States*, Carl Russell Fish, *The Rise of the Common Man*, Arthur M. Schlesinger, *New Viewpoints in American History*, Algie M. Simons, *Social Forces in American History*, and Leonard D. White, *The Jacksonians*; the

Mississippi Valley Historical Review for Edward Pessen, "The Workingmen's Movement of the Jacksonian Era"; the University of North Carolina Press for William H. Hoffman, *Andrew Jackson and North Carolina Politics*, Edwin A. Miles, *Jacksonian Democracy in Mississippi*, and Paul Murray, *The Whig Party in Georgia*; Oxford University Press for John W. Ward, *Andrew Jackson, Symbol for an Age*; Princeton University Press for Bray Hammond, *Banks and Politics in America*, and Lee Benson, *The Concept of Jacksonian Democracy*; the *Political Science Quarterly* for Edward Pessen, "Did Labor Support Andrew Jackson? The Boston Story," and William A. Sullivan, "Did Labor Support Andrew Jackson?"; Professor Henry H. Simms for *The Rise of the Whigs in Virginia, 1824-1840*; Stanford University Press for Marvin Meyers, *The Jacksonian Persuasion*, and Walter Hugins, *Jacksonian Democracy and the Working Class*; United States Publishers Association, sole distributors of the *Chronicles of America* series, for Frederic Austin Ogg, *The Reign of Andrew Jackson* (copyright Yale University Press); and Charles W. Wiltse for his *John C. Calhoun: Nullifier*.

UNIVERSITY OF FLORIDA MONOGRAPHS

Social Sciences

No. 1 (Winter 1959): *The Whigs of Florida, 1845-1854.* By Herbert J. Doherty, Jr.

No. 2 (Spring 1959); *Austrian Catholics and the Social Question, 1918-1933.* By Alfred Diamant

No. 3 (Summer 1959): *The Siege of St. Augustine in 1702.* By Charles W. Arnade

No. 4 (Fall 1959): *New Light on Early and Medieval Japanese Historiography.* By John A. Harrison

No. 5 (Winter 1960): *The Swiss Press and Foreign Affairs in World War II.* By Frederick H. Hartmann

No. 6 (Spring 1960): *The American Militia: Decade of Decision, 1789-1800.* By John K. Mahon

No. 7 (Summer 1960): *The Foundation of Jacques Maritain's Political Pholosophy.* By Hwa Yol Jung

No. 8 (Fall 1960): *Latin American Population Studies.* By T. Lynn Smith

No. 9 (Winter 1961): *Jacksonian Democracy on the Florida Frontier.* By Arthur W. Thompson

No. 10 (Spring 1961): *Holman Versus Hughes: Extension of Australian Commonwealth Powers.* By Conrad Joyner

No. 11 (Summer 1961): *Welfare Economics and Subsidy Programs.* By Milton Z. Kafoglis

No. 12 (Fall 1961): *Tribune of the Slavophiles: Konstantin Aksakov.* By Edward Chmielewski

No. 13 (Winter 1962): *City Managers in Politics: An Analysis of Manager Tenure and Termination.* By Gladys M. Kammerer, Charles D. Farris, John M. DeGrove, and Alfred B. Clubok

No. 14 (Spring 1962): *Recent Southern Economic Development as Revealed by the Changing Structure of Employment.* By Edgar S. Dunn, Jr.

No. 15 (Summer 1962): *Sea Power and Chilean Independence.* By Donald E. Worcester

No. 16 (Fall 1962): *The Sherman Antitrust Act and Foreign Trade.* By Andre Simmons

No. 17 (Winter 1963): *The Origins of Hamilton's Fiscal Policies.* By Donald F. Swanson

No. 18 (Spring 1963): *Criminal Asylum in Anglo-Saxon Law.* By Charles H. Riggs, Jr.

No. 19 (Summer 1963): *Colonia Barón Hirsch, A Jewish Agricultural Colony in Argentina.* By Morton D. Winsberg

No. 20 (Fall 1963): *Time Deposits in Present-Day Commercial Banking.* By Lawrence L. Crum

No. 21 (Winter 1964): *The Eastern Greenland Case in Historical Perspective.* By Oscar Svarlien

No. 22 (Spring 1964): *Jacksonian Democracy and the Historians.* By Alfred A. Cave